Devoted Friends

Amazing, True Stories About Animals Who Cared

Gretchen P. Alday

BETTERWAY PUBLICATIONS, INC.

WHITE HALL, VIRGINIA

Published by Shoe Tree Press, an imprint of
Betterway Publications, Inc.,
P.O. Box 219,
Crozet, VA 22932
(804) 823-5661

Cover design and cover photographs by Susan Riley
Typography by Park Lane Associates

Grateful acknowledgment is made for the use of the following material:
"Four-Feet," "Power of the Dog" and "His Apologies" © 1909, 1932 by Rud-
yard Kipling from *Rudyard Kipling's Verse: Definitive Edition*. Reprinted
by permission of The National Trust and Doubleday & Company, Inc.;
When The Snakes Awake: Animals and Earthquake Prediction, by Helmut
Tributsch; translated by Paul Langner. Published by the MIT Press, Cambridge, © 1982 by The Massachusetts Institute of Technology. Originally
published as *Wenn die Schlangen Erwachen*, © 1978 by Deutsche Verlags-
Anstalt GmbH, Stuttgart. Information used by permission of The MIT
Press; Excerpts from *Lassie-Come-Home*, by Eric Knight. Reprinted by permission of Curtis Brown, Ltd. ©, 1940 by Jere Knight. Copyright renewed
© 1968 by Jere Knight, Betty Noyes Knight, Winifred Knight Mewborn and
Jennie Knight Moore; Quotation from *Papa Hemingway: A Personal Memoir*, by A. E. Hotchner. New York: Random House, Inc., 1966. Used by permission of A. E. Hotchner.

Library of Congress Cataloging-in-Publication Data
Alday, Gretchen P.
    Devoted friends : amazing true stories about animals who cared
/ Gretchen P. Alday.
        p. cm.
    Includes bibliographical references.
    Summary: *A collection of over seventy anecdotes about extraor-
dinary behavior in animals, the animals of famous people throughout history and literature, and extrasensory perception in animals.*
    ISBN 1-55870-151-6 : $6.95
    1. Pets--Anecdotes--Juvenile literature. 2. Animals--Anecdotes--
Juvenile literature. 3. Animal heroes--Anecdotes--Juvenile literature.
4. Human-animal relationships--Juvenile literature. 5. Extrasensory
perception in animals--Juvenile literature. [1. Animals--Anecdotes. 2.
Pets--Anecdotes. 3. Extrasensory perception in animals.] I. Title.
SF416.A38 1990
636.088'7--dc20   89-29937
                                                            CIP
                                                            AC

Printed in the United States of America
0 9 8 7 6 5 4 3 2 1

For Bobbi (1967-1983), Lulu (1971-1983)
and Cowgirl (1973-1987)
the "original three," who taught me so much

And for the good people whose stories made this book possible
. . . especially the early contributors, who never lost faith.

Contents

Foreword

Devoted Friends is a celebration of our pets. The true stories in this book demonstrate the incredible sensitivity of our animals to all that goes on around them and highlight their intelligence and the many ways in which they enrich our lives.

The first story in Chapter One relates the incident which inspired me to write this book. My two dogs had been the best of friends for many years. When one died the other knew it, although they were separated by a great distance. If this experience had happened to my own "average pets," I thought, how many other people had stories to tell?

I contacted animal lovers across America and gathered a number of fascinating true stories. My faith in the human animal (sometimes shaky) was restored during this project. I'm convinced there are no better, more sensitive and caring people in the world than those who love and value their pets.

Writing *Devoted Friends* has been the most satisfying and fascinating experience of my life. It confirms what I have long suspected, which is that our pets offer us what humans often cannot: They don't care what we look like or how successful we are; they don't grow up and leave home; they don't divorce us; they are incapable of lying; and they seem ever willing to forgive us our mistakes. Animals are totally, wonderfully nonjudgmental.

I had no idea what kinds of true stories to expect when I began this book. As they came in, I couldn't help but notice some interesting similarities, such as the sameness of chosen words and described emotions used by the contributors when relating their stories. There seemed to be a common language among animal lovers.

I admire all animals; I'm not a breed snob, proclaiming one breed (or even one species) superior to others. Each and every animal is special, with its own personality and unique talents. I noticed, however, some intriguing patterns emerged as the stories arrived.

The dog stories, for instance, demonstrate that the retrievers, shepherds, and collies—and especially crosses of these breeds—are truly outstanding dogs. In one story after another, these dogs play sensitive and heroic roles.

I was delighted by the number of contributors of stories who have taken in drop/stray/abuse cases and have found them to be wonderful pets. Many of those with whom I corresponded on this project have discovered the joy and satisfaction of helping an animal in distress, whether saving it from an animal shelter, an abusive owner, or abandonment. And many have experienced perhaps an even greater satisfaction by having these animals spayed or neutered to help offset the overwhelming problem of pet overpopulation which contributed to these animals' sufferings in the first place.

The great ages of many pets in the stories was another impressive common denominator among the stories sent to me. It is heartening to know that many people feel gratitude and pride as their pets achieve senior citizen status. These people are right to be proud; the ages attained are a nice comment on the good care the pets have received at their hands.

This book wouldn't exist, of course, without the wonderful people—ranging from doctors and lawyers and artists to farmers and senior citizens and young girls—who allowed me to use stories about their animals in the book. I thank them with all my heart, especially the early contributors who never lost faith in me or the book.

PART ONE
Psychic Animals

"THE POWER OF THE DOG"
"GARM—A HOSTAGE"—ACTIONS AND REACTIONS
by Rudyard Kipling

There is sorrow enough in the natural way
From men and women to fill our day;
And when we are certain of sorrow in store,
Why do we always arrange for more?
Brothers and Sisters, I bid you beware
Of giving your heart to a dog to tear.

Buy a pup and your money will buy
Love unflinching that cannot lie—
Perfect passion and worship fed
By a kick in the ribs or a pat on the head.
Nevertheless it is hardly fair
To risk your heart for a dog to tear.

When the fourteen years which Nature permits
Are closing in asthma, or tumour, or fits,
And the vet's unspoken prescription runs
To lethal chambers or loaded guns,
Then you will find—it's your own affair—
But . . . you've given your heart to a dog to tear.

When the body that lived at your single will,
With its whimper of welcome, is stilled (how still!)
When the spirit that answered your every mood
Is gone—wherever it goes—for good,
You will discover how much you care,
And will give your heart to a dog to tear.

We've sorrow enough in the natural way,
When it comes to burying Christian clay.
Our loves are not given, but only lent,
At compound interest of cent per cent.
Though it is not always the case, I believe,
That the longer we've kept 'em, the more do we grieve:

For, when debts are payable, right or wrong,
A short-time loan is as bad as a long—
So why in—Heaven (before we are there)
Should we give our hearts to a dog to tear?

Chapter 1

ESP and Death

*A rooster crowing at the front door means
company is coming; a rooster crowing at
the back door means death is on the way.*
  —Animal superstition

I had a delightful little dog named Bobbi. A beagle-ter-rier crossbreed in appearance, she was mostly white with scattered brown patches and looked remarkably like Nipper, the RCA dog. I adopted Bobbi from a humane society in Florida and she was a wonderful pet—loving, loyal, and incredibly bright, with a happy and charming nature. I willingly "gave her my heart to tear."

Bobbi lived to be almost sixteen years old, and was in surprisingly good health until her last twenty-four hours. Then she disintegrated.

Early the next morning I took her on that last, long drive to the veterinarian to be euthanized. I thought much too highly of her to let her suffer and knew, with-out a doubt, the end was near. I left Cowgirl, my Aus-tralian shepherd, at home with my little boy and a baby-sitter. The two dogs, Bobbi and Cowgirl, had been the best of friends for ten years.

When I returned home from my heartbreaking mis-sion, I found the baby-sitter pale and shaken. "Bobbi died around eight o'clock, didn't she?" she asked.

"Yes," I said, puzzled.

The sitter told me that about a minute or two after eight, Cowgirl—who had been lying quietly at her feet—

suddenly jumped up and ran around and around the house, howling as though her heart were breaking. Cowgirl had known the moment her old friend died, and the vet's office was *twenty-five miles away*.

How did Cowgirl know her old friend had died? So often humans credit ESP experiences in animals to their highly superior senses of sight, hearing, and smell. But Cowgirl could not see, hear, or smell Bobbi.

Could her reaction have been the result of rising tension created by the people left at home with her as the hour of Bobbi's death approached? It's doubtful. My son was less than two years old at the time and had no idea what was happening. And the baby-sitter, although she knew the purpose of my trip to the vet, didn't know what time euthanasia would occur. Nor did I know; the vet's office had simply said to bring Bobbi over in the morning.

The sitter, absorbed in reading a book to my son, had not been watching the clock. It was Cowgirl's loud grief which caused her to look at the clock and note the time, in order to ask me about it.

I have no answer other than to say that Cowgirl was a special and remarkably sensitive dog. Just as some humans are more psychic than others, so are some animals.

Down through the years, in legend and in fact, dogs have shown a special sensitivity to death. It is believed in many parts of the world that a dog can see the approach of death, and a dog howling—particularly at night—is a warning that someone will soon die. A Mexican legend claims that a dog can see the Devil doing battle with guardian angels for the souls of dying people, and that is why dogs howl.[1]

Abraham Lincoln was known for his great tenderness toward all animals, and could understandably inspire devotion in a pet. It is said that his normally gentle dog went wild shortly *before* his assassination. The staff's attempts to calm the howling, mourning dog as he tore through the White House were to no avail.[2]

According to the memoirs of the Earl of Carnarvon, two bizarre incidents occurred when his father, Lord

Carnarvon, died in Cairo in 1922. Lord Carnarvon, the sponsor of the expedition that found the tomb of King Tutankhamen, died just a few months after his discovery. At the moment of his death, the lights in every section of Cairo went out, but no reason for the massive power failure was ever found. And, two thousand miles away in England, something else happened at that exact moment: Lord Carnarvon's favorite dog—a fox terrier named Susie—sat up in her basket, howled strangely, and fell back dead.[3]

What *is* ESP? The letters stand for "extrasensory perception," and refer to experiences that happen beyond the abilities of the normal, physical senses. The foreknowledge of Lincoln's unexpected death displayed by his dog and the instantaneous reaction of Lord Carnarvon's dog to his far-away demise would seem to be nothing else but ESP. Certainly sight, sound, or smell could not have played a role in these incidents.

Besides the ability to sense the passing of a beloved human or animal companion, some animals seem able to predict their own deaths.

Kris Crance of Clyde, New York, is a licensed animal health technician and works for a veterinarian. She gave a home to a Dalmatian named Rebel, who was a "hospital reject." He'd been hit by a car and sustained some head injuries; since he was no longer "perfect," his owners didn't want him anymore. He made a good recovery and Kris found him to be an excellent pet.

After living with Kris for many years, Rebel rather suddenly began to show his age. One evening he insisted on going into the living room with Kris, which was something he'd rarely done. He normally slept on a porch near a wood stove, and never seemed to desire any other accommodations.

"But that night he was persistent," remembers Kris, "almost as though he needed human contact." He climbed in Kris's lap and curled up—again, a most unusual thing for him to do.

The next day while Kris was at church, Rebel disappeared and was never seen again. Kris has always believed that Rebel knew it was their last time together, and he was saying good-bye.

Carol Strader, an animal lover from Middle Grove, New York, believes her cat, although perfectly healthy, knew he was going to die. Carol writes:

It seemed like the usual day around here. I was up early, fed the animals and then turned Rocko the dog and Weezee the cat outdoors for their normal playtime. They stayed out the whole day, and I didn't happen to glimpse them through the windows.

Suppertime came, and I went to the door to call them in. They stood close together at the bottom of the stairs, looking up at me with an expression on their faces I can only describe as sheepish. I called them again and, to my surprise, a small gray kitten wriggled forward from between them, almost as though the other two animals had been hiding him. Then all three rushed into the house.

Weezee took the kitten over to his food dish, and he and Rocko watched as the kitten ate his fill. Then Weezee ushered the kitten to the bedroom for a catnap, making the little fellow cozy on my comforter.

After the kitten's nap, Weezee took him on a tour of the rest of the house. They ended up in the living room, and Weezee introduced the kitten to the family.

The kitten stayed, of course—there was no way I could resist him. I named him Cody. I was amazed at how thoroughly and immediately he made himself at home.

For the next three days Rocko, Weezee and Cody were inseparable. Weezee continued to show Cody around, both indoors and out.

On the fourth morning, Weezee went out earlier than usual, leaving Cody asleep. We never saw Weezee again.

I believe Weezee knew that something was going to happen to him, and he brought us Cody to help us bear the pain of losing him. He must have loved us a lot to give us such a blessed gift. He made sure that Cody would fit into our family and lifestyle and that Rocko would get along with him. He took the time to show Cody the ropes before he left.

Cody is half-grown now and a real sweetheart. He is so like Weezee it's amazing. Both had big green eyes and both were tabbies, although Cody is gray and Weezee was a yellow tabby. Weezee was a very lovable cat, more like a dog. He came when you called him and lay down when you told him to. You could do anything with him—my children dressed him in doll clothes and carried him around like a baby. He was trusting and calm and especially loved to ride in the car. Cody acts the same, right down to going in the car.

We miss our Weezee a lot. We'll never forget him or the replacement he brought to the family he loved so much.

An eerie, historical story, associating a cat with the death of its owner, tells of the much-loved black cat belonging to England's King Charles I. It is said the cat went everywhere with King Charles, because the monarch believed it brought him luck. Then the cat died, and the distraught king wailed that his luck was gone. He was arrested the very next day and was later beheaded.[4]

Chapter 2

Disaster Predictions

But ask now the beasts, and they shall teach thee;
and the fowls of the air, and they shall tell thee.
—Job 12:7

Prudence K. Poppink, a California attorney living in Oakland, was a Peace Corps Volunteer in South America in the late 1960s. Pru was assigned to Cucuta, Colombia, and lived in a poor barrio for two years. Nearly everyone in the barrio had a fierce dog serving as a watch dog, and Pru herself had a black standard poodle named Schlingel (German for Rascal).

Pru went to bed as usual one night and was sleeping soundly when, around four o'clock in the morning, a bewildering racket jerked her awake. Every dog in the barrio was barking and howling with all its might, including her Schlingel. Within sixty seconds, a severe earthquake struck.

Georgia Bender, a writer/designer/poet from Kittanning, Pennsylvania, has contributed a great variety of stories to this book. In the first one, Georgia writes of a clairvoyant cat her family had when they were living in Iowa in 1947:

My mother's nineteen-pound, black-and-white cat Tommy was terrified of thunderstorms and would howl and hide during them. Eventually he would react if the sky merely clouded over or the wind came up.

One hot, bright day he went into his thunderstorm routine and cowered, trembling, as far back under the bed as he could go. But there was no wind, and the sky was a bright blue with few or no clouds.

Later we learned that at that exact time a tornado had passed through about ten miles north of town.

Barbara Milliken, an animal lover living in Greece, New York, enjoyed eleven fulfilling years with a sensitive Burmese named Cinnamon Toast of Walnut. Cinnamon was a cat who gave warning before earthquakes. When the two were living in California, the cat displayed great nervousness, ran around the house, and finally dashed under the bed to hide fifteen to twenty minutes before the chandelier-shaking tremors struck.

I have a horse who can predict the severity of a thunderstorm before it hits. Hudson is a thirty-five-year-old bay standardbred gelding. Coki, my other horse, is a nineteen-year-old palomino, half-Arab mare. The gelding is an honest, sensible old horse, while the mare is a little short on common sense. Fortunately, Hudson is the dominant horse and looks after Coki.

We can tell how bad an approaching thunderstorm is going to be by watching the horses. If the storm is going to be a severe one, with lightning bolts striking nearby, the old gelding herds the mare up to the barnyard and *makes* her stay there, much to her displeasure. If it's going to be a relatively mild storm, he allows her to remain in the pasture to graze and enjoy the natural bath provided by the rainfall.

All advancing storms look the same to us, with huge black clouds rolling in and the wind picking up. I don't know how Hudson knows which ones are going to be dangerous, but we trust his judgment to such an extent that if he herds Coki up to the barn at the beginning of a storm, we go and unplug the TV. Before we learned to depend on Hudson, we had a couple of televisions damaged by near strikes.

The great naturalist John James Audubon also had a horse whose intuitive judgment proved sound. Barro, a homely bay, had been taken from the wild by the Osage Indians and eventually sold to Audubon for fifty dollars. Audubon and Barro were on the last leg of a two-thousand-mile journey, a trip which hadn't fazed the tough little horse in the least, when Barro came to an abrupt stop and refused to go forward. Suddenly, the earth heaved and the trees tilted. Barro had known an earthquake was coming.[1]

The uncanny ability of animals to foretell earthquakes, hurricanes, avalanches, tidal waves, and volcanic eruptions has been known and recorded for centuries. The out-of-character behavior displayed by animals prior to earthquakes can take many forms: Horses whinny, break their halters, and flee the stables; dogs howl, bark without letup, and run off; cats' hair stands on end, and both cats and dogs have been known to remove their litters from buildings and take them out into the open. Ants (carrying their eggs) and bees leave their hills and hives in great agitation, chickens refuse to enter their coops, and snakes leave their burrows, even at risk of freezing in winter.

When the Snakes Awake: Animals and Earthquake Prediction, a fascinating and detailed book written by Helmut Tributsch (The MIT Press, 1982), describes one incident after another of abnormal animal behavior minutes—or even hours—before earthquakes. Early records report a mass exodus of animals days before an earthquake destroyed Helice, Greece in 373 B.C., an earthquake of such magnitude that the city disappeared into the sea.

Tributsch has compiled extensive tables showing the sites of earthquakes, the intensities (where recording was possible), the nature of the abnormal behavior of the animals, and the length of time preceding the earthquake that this behavior was first noticed. He also includes a table which compares the behavior of animals before dramatic weather changes to their behavior before earthquakes; the behavior is virtually the same.

In some countries, most notably China, animal behavior is routinely observed as a means of early earthquake detection and has been proven to save lives. For a while the United States had a Project Earthquake Watch, federally funded and based in California, which involved a large group of people who observed many species of animals for signs of abnormal behavior prior to earthquakes.

How are animals able to predict earthquakes? There are many theories, including the possibility that odors escape from the ground, the occurrence of minute movements of the earth, the changes in the magnetic field that take place, or the static charges that are produced prior to earthquakes.

In ancient times, the ability of animals to predict natural disasters was considered "supernatural." In reality, animals' predictive powers are almost certainly due to their senses being extraordinarily sensitive to physical changes in the world around them, rather than ESP.

Besides predicting natural disasters, animals can anticipate man-made catastrophes as well. In World War I the English government conscripted five hundred thousand cats who were able to warn of the approach of poison gas well before humans could detect it. They saved many lives.

And in World War II British cats were able to sense the approach of enemy bombers before even radar could detect them. Hair on end, the cats made a beeline for bomb shelters, and smart humans immediately followed. Because cats were believed to have saved so many English lives in this way, they were awarded a special medal engraved with the words: We Also Serve.

Cats' ears are attuned to higher frequencies of sound than humans. (Interestingly, I've read that this might be one reason cats are more responsive to women's voices than to men's.) In the London bombings, it's probable that the cats' specialized ears heard the high whine of the aircraft and they developed a conditioned response to that particular sound: i.e., that sound was followed by bombing and death.

Seagulls are also reported to be highly sensitive to warplanes. In war-torn areas they take to the air, crying shrilly, long before humans have any idea of approaching danger.[2]

Whatever the reason, animals often know about impending natural and unnatural disasters beforehand, and we don't. This gift has proven to be of great benefit to humans who notice, and heed, the signs.

Chapter 3

Homing and Psi-Trailing

*An empty house is like a stray dog or a body
from which life has departed.*
—Samuel Butler

One of the most famous stories of all time about an animal's homing ability is *Lassie-Come-Home*, the wonderful classic written by the late Eric Knight. In this moving story the collie named Lassie is separated from the young boy she loves and is taken hundreds of miles away to Scotland. The beautiful and intelligent dog escapes her new home to make the tortuous journey back to the boy. Eric Knight wrote:

> Lifting her head again, as the desire for her true home woke in her, she scented the breeze as if asking directions. Then, without hesitation, she struck down the road to the south. Do not ask any human being to explain how she should know this. Perhaps, thousands upon thousands of years ago, before man "educated" his brain, he too had the same homing sense; but if he had it, it is gone now. Not with all his brain development can man tell how a bird or an animal can be crated, taken miles away in darkness, and when released, strike straight back toward its home. Man only knows that animals can do what he can neither do himself nor explain.

Although *Lassie-Come-Home* is fiction, Eric Knight demonstrates a singular feeling throughout the book for the senses of an animal. He was probably right, too, about humans possessing a homing ability long ago. Many scientists believe that primitive humans had more highly developed senses than people today, simply because they needed them to survive. Our senses seem to have blunted as our intellects developed.

A true homing ability is believed to be possessed even today by less "civilized" groups of people, such as the Pygmies of the Congo. When tested, Pygmies have proven exceptionally good at homing.[1]

Pigeons, of course, have long been known to excel at homing. The first Duke of Wellington, born in the 1760s, released a pigeon from a sailing vessel off the coast of West Africa. Fifty-five days later, the bird plummeted to the earth, dead, very near its home in London. The distance involved was five thousand to seven thousand miles, depending on the air route taken.[2]

Cats are also excellent at homing. Mary F. Hassett, a friend from Scottsville, New York, tells the following true homing story:

> About sixty years ago, we had a stray kitten come to our farmhouse. Her long hair was tan and yellow and black, and she seemed to be about five months old. My mother was very compassionate and fed the poor little stray, much to the disgust of our resident cat. We named the stray Kitty.
>
> A few months later, my uncle Ed came to visit from Bliss, a hamlet about fifty miles from us. In the course of conversation, he said his barn was overrun with mice. Mother offered Kitty to him as she knew my uncle would be kind to her. He accepted and put Kitty in a burlap bag on the floor of his car. Fifty miles away, she was turned out in his barn.
>
> The next morning when Uncle Ed went to take her some milk, she darted out and was gone. He wrote to my mother and said he was so sorry.
>
> Kitty's escape should be the end of the story, but it isn't. One month later, my mother opened the door to a

very emaciated and fur-matted cat, who rubbed around her feet and purred. Mother couldn't believe her eyes.

Kitty was back, and my parents said if she wanted a home with us that badly, she deserved it. She lived with us the remainder of her twelve years.

To this day, I still wonder how she did it.

That's a good question. Homing is the ability of non-migratory animals—such as dogs, cats, and pigeons—to find their way back to familiar territory after they have become lost. No one knows exactly how animals do it. Somehow—perhaps by scent, visual clues, the position of the sun, or the earth's magnetism (this last being the most accepted theory)—they know how to get home. When tested, even kittens whose eyes have not yet opened can find their way back to their nests from several feet away, although this ability is thought to be due to smell.[3]

Dr. Robert Brooks, an anesthesiologist living in Oakland, California, and his wife, attorney Dale Brodsky, had an exceptional dog named Piglet, who used his homing ability for his own special ends.

Bob got Piglet from a pound in Palo Alto when the dog was just a young pup. The shaggy black and white dog matured to look like a small bearded collie. He displayed an uncanny intelligence at times and, Dale says, "was very independent, very much his own dog."

When Bob and Dale began dating, they both lived in San Francisco, and their apartments were located about two miles apart (Dale on Edgewood Street, Bob and Piglet on Sacramento). One day Bob and Dale had a terrible fight and decided to end their relationship.

Two days later Piglet, all on his own, showed up at Dale's apartment. She was amazed; Piglet had been driven to her place prior to that, but had never walked there. He'd crossed two miles of downtown San Francisco to find her.

Dale, of course, had to call Bob to let him know about Piglet, and the phone call led to a reconciliation. Since the relationship obviously had Piglet's stamp of approval, how could they do less than marry?

When Bob did his internship at Mt. Zion Hospital, he sometimes took Piglet with him, rather than leave the dog home alone. Bob placed food and water in the car and left the window rolled down to allow Piglet to jump out if he had to relieve himself.

One day when Bob and Piglet arrived home from the hospital, Bob's neighbor exclaimed with surprise, "I thought you were home today! Piglet was here."

Bob learned that Piglet had jumped out the car window and returned home to Sacramento Street, a mile and a half trip from the hospital through San Francisco. According to the neighbor, the dog had played and romped the day away and had eaten a meal. Piglet then returned to Bob's car in the hospital parking lot, jumped back through the car window, and was innocently waiting when Bob finished work. Bob would never have known how his dog spent the day if the neighbor hadn't seen Piglet and squealed.

For Piglet to jump out the window, find his way home along a busy route filled with dangers and distractions, enjoy himself once there, and then return to the car before he was missed demonstrates such intelligence, resourcefulness, homing ability (for both his home and a car in a parking lot), and sense of timing as to be astounding. Piglet lived to be fifteen years old, and Dale and Bob's grief at his death is easily understood.

Most of us could verify that our pets know where they're going when riding in vehicles, even if they don't look out the window. Dottie Hilvers, of Cincinnati, Ohio, shares the following story:

Our gray and brown striped cat, Simon, lived seventeen and a half years. He was extremely sensitive and very cautious. When we'd put him in the car, he'd shiver and shake all the way to the vet, whose office was a mile from our house. Beyond the vet's office, after turning a corner, my parents' home is another mile down the road. When taking Simon to my parents', he'd cower and shake until we passed the vet's office and turned that corner. Then for the next mile he'd be calm and peer out the window. He seemed to sense that the destination would then be pleasant.

It is said that seafaring animals are able to sense in which direction land lies, and this ability has long been appreciated by sailors. It was mainly for this reason that ships, in the days before sophisticated equipment, kept a cat on board. The cat tended to favor the side of the vessel nearest home.[4]

A fascinating and supposedly true Black Stallion-type story about an animal sensing land from water is that of a seventeen-hand thoroughbred gelding named Moifaa. According to the story, Moifaa was being transported by ship from his home in New Zealand to England. Off the coast of Ireland, he was either swept overboard in a violent storm or shipwrecked (versions of this story differ in many aspects), and it was assumed he had perished.

Somehow, the horse managed to swim one hundred miles to land and was found on a beach by some fishermen. Not long after, and not in the best of condition, this great-hearted thoroughbred won the 1904 Grand National, England's challenging steeplechase race. It is said King Edward VII was so impressed with Moifaa's story and accomplishments that he bought him for his personal mount.

Homing is an impressive instinct, but trailing (or psi-trailing, the psi referring to an unexplainable communication) is another situation altogether and appears to be a true ESP phenomenon. In psi-trailing cases the animal's family moves to a different locale (sometimes hundreds or even thousands of miles away) and either leaves the pet behind or loses the pet en route to the new home. The pet somehow finds the owner at the new location which has never before been visited by the animal.

This seems impossible, and yet it happens. It can take months or years for the animal to find its family, and heaven only knows what hardships it's faced along the way. Since the animal has never before been in the area, none of its normal senses would be of help in locating the family. It would seem the only "magnetism" involved in trailing cases is that of love for the humans the animals want so desperately to rejoin.

An historical story of trailing is that of a cat belonging to the Earl of Southamptom. This cat searched out his beloved human after the Earl was jailed in the infamous Tower of London. It is said the cat, once he found the Earl, joined him by descending the chimney of his chamber.

A modern-day trailing story is contributed by Susan Martin, a horse breeder/dog groomer from Burgin, Kentucky, who says this incident made her a believer in ESP:

Our family had a small, brown spitz-like mongrel who came to us as a stray. I was about two years old when Brownie became a member of our family. At the time we lived in a farmhouse in Halloway, Michigan.

Every summer Brownie would go with us on our summer vacation. One summer we went to Florida, arriving in the late afternoon at the end of three days of road travel. There were five members in my family, and we decided to split up for our visit; some of us would stay in St. Petersburg, and some would go over to Gulfport—a fifteen minute drive away—to my other grandparents' home.

I spent the night at our original destination and had Brownie with me. I walked him after dinner and, as I entered the house and took off his lead, he bolted out the door and headed full-speed down the street. After hours of searching and calling, we decided to wait till morning to search further. We hoped maybe he'd return by then.

The next morning, after a sleepless night and a lot of worrying, I searched again . . . but no dog. I was heartbroken, and the vacation was ruined.

Then a miracle happened, and I'm sure it was just that. Brownie showed up on the doorstep of the other grandparents' home—fifteen minutes away by car! The incredible thing was that *he'd never been there before*; the grandparents had just moved in that year.

Brownie was safe and sound, and the family was ecstatic. He lived to enjoy many more vacations and his sixteenth birthday. He was a wonderful pet and influenced me to spend a lifetime in animal occupations.

A famous, and verified, case of psi-trailing, which appears in many books about animals, is the story of Pigeon 167. A twelve-year-old boy made a pet of a pigeon who showed up in his backyard one day. The pigeon's leg was banded with the number 167.

In 1939, the boy needed an operation, and was taken to a hospital about a hundred miles away by car, although considerably less by air. It's known that the pigeon didn't follow the vehicle transporting the boy; the bird was seen at home during the time the youngster was taken to the hospital.

One blustery, snowy night about a week later, the boy saw an agitated pigeon at the window of his room in the hospital. He asked a nurse to let the bird in and, when she did, told her to read the band on the pigeon's leg. The band proved it was Pigeon 167.

For an animal to succeed at homing or psi-trailing, it must possess great motivation, a good deal of intelligence and resourcefulness, and a lot of luck. Think what the animal must overcome: traffic, fences, bodies of water, humans who will use any method to drive off (or capture) a stray, hostilities of other animals whose territory they invade, hunters looking for target practice, lack of food, rugged terrain, and pure physical exhaustion. Of these, traffic is by far the most dangerous obstacle, since all traveling animals (except birds) must eventually cross a road or travel the shoulder. The animal—hungry, with sore pads, and too tired to be alert—is seldom able to stay clear of speeding vehicles.

The miracle is that *any* pet makes it to the end of its "journey of the heart."

Chapter 4

Grieving Animals

He prayeth well who loveth well
Both man and bird and beast.
—Samuel Taylor Coleridge

A Celtic legend tells of Cuchulainn, who was stabbed by betrayers and then tied to a stone slab with his belt so that he might die standing up. Cuchulainn's black horse approached just before his master died, nuzzled him, and walked away crying real tears.[1]

According to Greek mythology, Achilles's horses also cried in grief. Dun-colored Xanthus and dappled Balius were beautiful horses with long, flowing manes. On the Trojan battlefield, Achilles lent his magnificent horses and chariot to Patroclus, who was killed. The horses were deeply grieved. They stood apart from battle, heads hung low, and tears flowed down their lovely faces, soaking the ground beneath them.

Sorrow in an animal is not a myth, as I'm sure many readers of this book could confirm from their own experiences. The following story was written by Carol Beasley Strader from Middle Grove, New York, who asked that it be dedicated to Mr. Beasley and Buddy Jack:

My daddy bought Buddy when he was a five-month-old colt. We raised and trained him together, but Buddy was my dad's treasure, his pride. Buddy was part quarter horse and part thoroughbred, sorrel in color with a white star. He matured to 14.3 hands and weighed 1,133 pounds. Buddy was an all-round youth and adult horse, and I showed him in western stock classes.

My daddy passed away in 1979, after a two-year battle with cancer. At that time Buddy was seventeen years old. The day of the funeral, we had to travel past our farm to the church. As the funeral procession went by our home, we could see our horses in the pasture—and there was Buddy, watching us.

At the church service our preacher talked of my father's love for horses and of Buddy and of our farm setting. After the funeral we returned to our home.

That afternoon at the usual time, I went out to feed the horses. I let all of them in; each of them knew which stall was theirs and went straight into it to eat. Buddy had the number one stall, up front by the big double doors to the entrance of the barn.

Instead of going into his stall to eat as he always did, Buddy passed his stall and walked slowly to the big double front doors, which were slightly open. He stuck his head and massive neck out through the doors and looked down the road toward the church and cemetery grounds. He stood there looking for several minutes, then slowly backed up, turned and, with his head carried so low that his nose nearly touched the ground, walked ever so slowly to his stall.

Buddy still didn't go to his food. He stood in the corner of his stall, facing a back wall, grieving for his friend of many years.

I went into his stall and put my arms around his neck, trying to comfort him. I kissed Buddy's cheek and then saw that he was *crying*. Tears were running down his sorrel face. We cried together.

From that day on, Buddy never again went right into his stall to eat. He always went first to the big double doors and looked down the road to the cemetery, as if saying, "I'll never forget you, my friend."

Georgia Bender's father also had an animal who deeply mourned his human's passing. Her father owned a devoted beagle named Charlie, who was considered by the family to be the smartest dog in the world. Georgia writes:

Charlie could not endure to be left behind and usually retaliated ("Well, they went off without Charlie, so he got on the table and chewed up your mother's hat"), but they took him along whenever possible. He joined in the social gatherings, rode in the car, and loved to go fishing.

My father had a heart condition that caused him much pain but eluded diagnosis. Actually it was a flaw in his aorta, which swelled and strained at times, but appeared normal during tests. So my father continued with a normal life, and one fine day (May 1, 1965, to be precise) he went fishing with some friends, taking Charlie along with him to the fishing cabin.

They had a glorious time preparing their boats for the new season. But after dinner that evening, as they sat playing cards and drinking beer, my father complained of pain and finally said, "This really is a heart attack."

His friends got him to the car and drove back to town at high speed, Charlie whining beside him on the back seat. As they pulled into the hospital parking lot my father said, "Oh, my God," and died. The aorta had torn loose.

When attendants came to the car, Charlie sat on my father's chest and snarled, defying anyone to reach in. Nowadays that would waste precious seconds, but medicine was far more limited then and this was a small-town hospital; nothing could have been done.

The next few days, Charlie paced the apartment endlessly, barking and howling. Then he began trying to bite anyone who entered. My mother had Charlie humanely euthanized by a veterinarian ... the only way that, this time, Charlie could "go too."

Georgia Bender contributes another interesting story, which adds an overtone of guilt to an animal's grief:

Our cat Daisy was a true Manx. She was soft-spoken, timid yet playful, but for her, rough stuff was unthinkable. If a ball bounced against Daisy, she left the room. Drop a book, and Daisy was convinced it was thrown at her.

Another of our cats, Doodad, however, had the energetic spirit of his mixed tabby-Siamese background. Whenever Daisy sat on a table looking out the window, Doodad loved to sneak up behind and nip her twitching little one-joint tail.

This always infuriated her, but other games began to loosen her up. It even began to look as though Daisy might forget her proper Manx upbringing, especially when we saw her romp about the house with Doodad on a few occasions.

One evening she even waited excitedly, crouching by the basement door and, when Doodad came up, bopped him over the head with both paws.

Unfortunately, that was the night that Doodad got out of the house and disappeared. We searched for several days, and some of the neighbors joined in, but it was February with deep snow on the ground. We never saw Doodad again. He could not have survived long, yet it was a success story of sorts for freedom was what he, a feral kitten, had always wanted.

I grieved, but not nearly as much as Daisy. She called and squeaked pathetically and searched for him for weeks, looking in all his favorite spots, dark corners, and down all the cold air registers.

She never played rough games again. Knowing the Manx, I'm sure Daisy blamed herself ... seeing her game and his loss as cause and effect.

Grief in animals has been studied to some extent, and it was found that grieving behavior usually lasts two or three days in birds and several days longer in mammals. After that time, the animal either returns to normal or dies.[2]

My Aussie, Cowgirl (mentioned in Chapter One), was depressed for weeks after Bobbi died. She was unusually quiet, had little appetite, and clung to my side wherever I went.

We grieved together, and it was oddly comforting to know that another living being shared my pain. Certainly no other human did. We'd both lost a dear friend. I understood how she felt, and she seemed to understand how I felt. We helped each other through a bad time.

Chapter 5

Communicating with Animals

Nature teaches beasts to know their friends.
—William Shakespeare

To return to *Lassie-Come-Home* for a moment, on her long journey home the weary collie was befriended for a time by Pedlar Palmer. The day came when Lassie had to leave him and go her own way again, and as he said good-bye to her she responded to certain words with barks and tail waggings. The pedlar said, "Nay, that's the pity of it. Ye can understand some o' man's language, but man isn't bright enough to understand yours. And yet it's us that's supposed to be the most intelligent!"

It's possible that humans were once bright enough to understand the language of animals. Native American Indians spoke of animals as their brothers. In fact, the Cherokee believed that long, long ago, animals were much bigger and more powerful than they are today. The animals of those days possessed supernatural powers and were able to perform miracles. And they spoke the same language as man.

Another such story, that of Balaam's ass, appears in the Bible (Numbers 22). Three times the ass carrying Balaam saw the angel of the Lord, sword in hand, blocking their passage. Three times she turned aside, and three times Balaam struck her with a staff for doing so. The ass opened her mouth and reproached Balaam for striking her, proclaiming her loyalty to him. Then God revealed the armed angel to Balaam, and he understood the ass had saved his life. Some people believe this story was meant to display God's power in caring for us, even making the animals talk to carry out His plans.

Georgia Bender, from Kittanning, Pennsylvania, had an experience with her cat, Sputty, which makes you wonder if our pets sometimes forget to keep the barriers up between us and them:

> My husband switched off the television as the news ended and said, "Come on, Sputty. Time to go out." Which was too bad, for the night was cold. But cats are nocturnal and an in-and-outer like Sputty is most active at night. This year, however, since the weather had turned to winter, Sputty had taken to hiding under the bed when the news neared completion. This night he was crouched pathetically on the far side of the room looking at us, sadly, it seemed. Then:
>
> "I OH AHN OO."
>
> The voice was high and strange, but the meaning was unmistakably clear (try saying it over to yourself a few times until it runs together). Actually, the speech was much clearer than that of many children. My husband and I stared at each other, then began to exclaim, "Did he—? Did you hear?"
>
> Sputty suddenly looked away, hung his head, and scurried to the door, refusing to let us touch him, impatient to get outside, as though he had committed a horrible sin. He probably had.

Our primary communication with animals is through body language, and animals use their bodies to communicate with one another and with us. Few humans are sensitive and knowledgeable enough to read and correctly interpret an animal's body signals, although this situation is steadily improving, thanks to a number of excellent books on the subject which have been published in recent years.

Animals, on the other hand, can read humans like a book. The old saying that dogs can detect fear is true. Fear, kindness, compassion, sorrow, joy, worry, good intentions and bad, are all known, immediately and effortlessly, by animals.

To an animal, our emotions literally *smell*. Combined with our smells are voice characteristics, facial expressions, tense or relaxed body movements, and any number of other physical clues that scream out our innermost thoughts. Animals are highly sensitive to physical nuances; they need barely glance at or sniff us to see what stuff we're made of, and to differentiate between friend or foe.

This ability is true not only of domestic animals, but of wild animals as well. Someone enjoying a simple nature walk is apt to see many more wild animals than a hunter, even if the latter is not carrying a weapon, but only out to scout the game in an area. Wild animals seem even better at determining human motives than our domestic friends, and with good reason: Judging accurately means life or death.

I have noticed animals sometimes act differently around children than they do around adults. On a number of occasions, I've seen otherwise feisty horses tuck in their chins and calmly, with exaggerated care, give a small child a safe ride. And many cats and dogs will allow a young child to clamber over them and pull their tails or ears, whereas an adult trying the same thing would be quickly punished.

Margaret Yarbrough, an animal lover from Auburn, Alabama, recalls a retired racehorse who was very considerate of two little girls:

My father had a thousand-acre farm when I was growing up, and the nearest school was more than six miles away. I was seven and my sister, Marian, was eleven, and we needed a safe way to get to and from school. My father picked up a retired racehorse in Kentucky, brought her home, and trained her to pull a buggy in order to transport us. Her name was Boots, and she was chestnut brown with four white feet and a star in the middle of her forehead.

Boots did a wonderful job; she knew exactly where she was going, how to get there, and needed no direction. Well-supplied with food and a watering trough, she spent the days in a lot behind the school.

Boots could have run off with my sister and me any time she chose, but the faith my parents placed in her was justified. One day on the way home from school, a strap on Boots's harness broke. She stopped dead, wouldn't move, and stood looking back at us. We tried laying the broken strap on her back, but she still refused to getty-up. Boots stood fast until help arrived to fix the strap properly.

When animals recognize juvenility in humans, they are probably noting the round faces, smaller sizes, and clumsy movements typical of all young animals. Or they could simply be reacting to an aura of nonaggression, since animals often respond to large, adult-looking teenagers with the same benevolence they afford small children.

A well-known legend in Christian folklore of a cat's good will toward a child is the story of the little gray tabby who comforted the baby Jesus as he lay unable to sleep in the manger one night. Mary asked all the animals in the stable for help in lulling him to sleep, but none succeeded. Finally, a small tabby came forward, licked itself clean, leaped lightly next to the infant and lulled the baby to sleep with its purring. It is said tabbies ever since have had the letter M on their foreheads in token of the Madonna's gratitude.

Besides children, there are certain special adults who are treated kindly by all beasts. These people seem to have a natural affinity with all of nature, and animals are drawn to them.

A famous example coming immediately to mind is St. Francis of Assisi. An unusual man, St. Francis overflowed with an innocent and joyous love of God and nature. He referred to animals as his "little brothers and sisters."

There was something about St. Francis which caused creatures to love and respect him. Never was he harmed by an animal, not even the infamous Wolf of Gubbio.

The citizens of Gubbio lived in terror of a huge wolf who regularly attacked those who ventured beyond the town gates. One day St. Francis arrived and calmly walked out of the gates to confront the wolf who gave a blood-curdling howl and ran toward the kindly man. Francis marched steadily forward to meet him, made the sign of the cross over the wolf, and had a talk with him. Incredibly, the wolf appeared to heed his words for, instead of attacking, he wagged his tail and bowed his head.

St. Francis asked the wolf to mend his evil ways, and it is said the wolf signaled his agreement by placing his big paw in the hand the man offered him. St. Francis led the wolf into Gubbio, where he became the well-fed pet of all the townspeople.[1]

St. Francis is best known for preaching to the birds. On one occasion, all the birds in the area congregated in an open field and listened in perfect silence as this special man spoke words of love. Even when he walked among them and his habit touched them, they did not fly off. Legend has it that they flew away only after he finished his sermon and told them to depart.

The lark was St. Francis's favorite kind of bird. As St. Francis was dying, a large group of singing larks descended and whirled above the cell in which he lay. Their actions were remarkable because the birds came at dusk, and larks normally sing only in the early morning.[2]

There are several fascinating stories concerning animals and Paderewski, the enormously talented Polish pianist. One such story tells of Paderewski's nervousness preceding a concert debut in London. When he sat down to play the opening number, a cat jumped onto his lap and remained, purring, until he finished the piece. Everyone was charmed by this, and it is said Paderewski credited that cat with getting his career off to a good start.[3]

With what we know today about the calming benefits of animals—including the fact that simply stroking a pet can immediately lower blood pressure—it's understandable that the cat in the theater helped the brilliant pianist relax and play well.

Did the cat sense the nervous pianist's turmoil, or was it simply attracted to the music? Animals often respond pleasurably to music and, evidently, Paderewski's playing could charm all sorts of creatures—even spiders.

According to the story, a spider living in the pianist's home dropped down from above and hung suspended just above the piano every time he played a particular Chopin etude. Any other music sent the tiny arachnid scurrying back up to the ceiling.[4]

Jenny Lind (The Swedish Nightingale), the gifted coloratura soprano, owes her career to a cat who enjoyed listening to her sing. Pussy was a big, handsome cat and was a loyal listener as nine-year-old Jenny sang to her in the windowsill. A young servant girl heard Jenny singing to the cat and told her mistress—a famous dancer—about Jenny's beautiful voice. The dancer had Jenny sing for her. Highly impressed, she insisted Jenny audition at the Royal Theater, and the rest is history.[5]

Jeanne Huenefeld, an animal lover from Cincinnati, Ohio, had a turtle who responded to music. His name was Tripod, and he was originally a "dime store" turtle. Due to an injury, Tripod had only three legs, but the only real trouble it caused him was that he had a harder time righting himself than other turtles if he was turned upside down.

With the help of a herpetologist, Jeanne and her family learned how to take good care of Tripod. They had him for many years, and he grew to be very large.

The family piano, kept in the den where Tripod lived, was played daily. Each day as soon as the music began,

Tripod scurried onto his rock pile and stretched his neck out as far as it would go, as though he didn't want to miss hearing a note. When the music stopped, he scampered down and resumed swimming.

Music and kindly auras aside, can we communicate with our animals verbally? There is some belief that we can actually explain things to our pets when they are upset, and that this consideration has a calming effect on them. The words themselves are probably not understood, but somehow our message gets across.

Georgia Bender, of Kittanning, Pennsylvania, writes the following experience:

> When my husband had to go away on business, Poppy, a silver tabby, stopped speaking to my daughter and me. Later, when my husband was hospitalized, Poppy became progressively upset, so when phoning him at the hospital, we'd say, "Now say something nice to the kitty," and we would put the phone to Poppy's ear.
>
> Whatever my husband said, Poppy would turn and look at the phone in amazement and then seem much more at ease the rest of the evening.

A classic, rose-gray Arabian stallion named Marnyhym proved that he understood exactly what was said around him. He was owned for most of his life by Kay Wilcox, who now lives in Tucson, Arizona.

Kay did everything with this versatile horse. She used Marny for trail riding, showed him in performance and halter classes, bred him extensively, and even barrel-raced him. Kay and Marny had an especially close relationship, but the day came when Kay, who was phasing out of Arabs and going into quarter horses, made the difficult decision to sell him.

A woman came from California to look Marny over and try him out. Not surprisingly, she fell in love with him and made arrangements with Kay to buy him, agreeing to come back in thirty days to pick him up.

When the deal was struck, the two women were standing in front of Marny's stall. He heard it all.

That day the magnificent horse stopped eating and remained off his feed day after day. "Every test known to man was done," recalls Kay, "and showed nothing physically wrong with him." But Marny was dying.

Kay knew her horse. She finally went to his stall, sobbing, and had a talk with him. She told Marny that if it would kill him to be sold, she wouldn't do it. She promised to cancel the whole deal and not let him go.

"He began eating immediately," says Kay. "Within hours he started coming back."

If animals heed our words, then turn about is fair play. In ancient Saxon legend, a horse's voice decided the fate of a nation. It was believed the gods used horses as mediums of expression. Great attention was paid to their neighing, in case it conveyed a message. The Persians had to select a king in 521 B.C., and all those competing for the title met on horseback at the appointed time. The horses were to decide: The man whose horse whinnied first would be chosen king. Darius's horse won the honor for him, and history proclaims him an excellent ruler.[6]

Chapter 6

Unexplainable Stories

*A person passes into the body of a cat
at the moment of death.*
—African belief

Do animals return from the dead?

Sometimes people swear a pet they have now is so like one they had before that it *has* to be that same animal reincarnated. Their observation is understandable, because much species behavior is identical; most cats will do certain things in certain situations, as will most dogs.

People will point out that the special spot a deceased animal used to lie on is the same one favored now by the new pet. But that's not unusual; the scent of the first pet could remain, or the spot could be one that would naturally appeal to the new pet, for example, if the spot were near a heat source or is a central place from which the animal can keep an eye on its human.

However, actions truly unique to the deceased pet, which are later exhibited by the new animal, are harder to explain. Barbara Milliken, an animal lover living in Greece, New York, has two cats, a Siamese and a ten-month-old Burmese named Chan of Apreskhat.

These cats greatly enjoy watching television. Chan, the Burmese, turns it on himself when the mood strikes. Many a time, Barbara has returned from shopping to find the television blaring and both cats comfortably settled on the love seat facing it. The last time this happened, Barbara says, they were watching a Mickey

Mouse cartoon.

Barbara's first Burmese was Cinnamon Toast of Walnut (mentioned in Chapter Two), a cat she dearly loved and had for eleven years. Cinnamon died in 1987, and Barbara searched for another Burmese for two years before finding Chan.

What amazes Barbara is that Cinnamon, the first Burmese, also enjoyed television, and regularly turned it on. The first time she came home to find the set blaring after Chan came, Barbara couldn't believe her eyes. The Siamese has never turned it on, but Cinnamon often turned it on in Barbara's presence, as does Chan.

"Chan has so many of the same little tricks Cinnamon had it almost seems like reincarnation," Barbara says. When Barbara bends over to brush her teeth in the bathroom, for instance, Chan jumps up and drapes himself across her shoulders, just exactly as Cinnamon used to.

Turning on and watching television and draping themselves on humans while they brush their teeth does not qualify as the normal species behavior of cats.

Sammy, a cocker spaniel belonging to Mary Jo Brown, a speech pathologist now living in Rochester, New York, provided a real service to his humans. Sammy was the family dog when Mary Jo was growing up.

His special brand of helpfulness was to go on point *before* the telephone rang. This was truly appreciated by his family. Mary Jo's father was a physician, and there were three office phones as well as two house phones in their home. It was confusing and difficult for the humans to tell which one was ringing.

A moment or two before it happened, Sammy moved toward whichever telephone was going to ring. His ears perked, his tail (such as it was) rose, his body tensed, and he raised his paw in a classic point toward the phone, which then rang. He was always right.

Cowgirl, my Australian shepherd, also provided her family with a helpful service. When my husband and I were farming, and I was out picking apples each autumn in the block of trees behind the house (a distance of from twenty-five to a hundred and seventy-five yards, depending on where I was picking), I never worried about Chris, my little boy, asleep upstairs in the house. His naps could last anywhere from a half hour to three-and-a-half-hours. Rather than lose valuable picking time by running back and forth to the house to check on Chris, I depended on Cowgirl.

She stayed near me when I picked. When Chris woke up, Cowgirl somehow knew it; she rushed up to me, managing to convey both excitement and worry. I'd say, "Oh, he's up now, is he?" and head for the house, with Cowgirl urging me forward by running back and forth between me and the door. Invariably, as I walked through the door, Chris was just coming down the stairs.

In the above stories about Sammy and Cowgirl, it's possible that their seemingly "supernatural" actions were the result of the exceptional acuity of their hearing. Sammy might have been able to hear a slight click or buzz, inaudible to humans, on the line before the telephone rang. And Cowgirl—even at a great distance— might have heard Chris's happy babble as he awoke from his nap. Regardless of how they managed these feats, they were able to know things we couldn't and were a great help to us.

We often hear of supernatural events involving dogs and cats, but horses seem to have their fair share of otherworldly connections too. From a winged horse (Pegasus) to horned horses (unicorns) to the many angel horses in the Bible, horses figure heavily in mythology and legend. In the second book of Kings 2:11, Elisha and Elijah were parted when ". . . there appeared a chariot of fire, and horses of fire, and parted them both asunder; and Elijah went up by a whirlwind into heaven."

In America the Plains Indians, like the Blackfoot, built an entire new culture with the arrival of the horse. Horses improved the quality of their lives to such an extent it seemed they must be a gift of the gods.

A great rapport existed between Indian and horse as a result of shared experiences in hunting and war. When a Blackfoot Indian's horse died, he would sometimes weep publicly, and if the Indian died first, the mane and tail of the deceased's horse was often cut short to demonstrate its mourning for the owner.

The feats made possible by the Indian pony's strength and endurance seemed almost miraculous. It was believed that some horses possessed supernatural powers, and could survive death as spirits. The powerful Horse Medicine Cult began when horses appeared to their owners in dreams and conferred their powers on individual Indians.[1]

Supernatural events involving horses still happen today. The last two stories in this Psychic Animals section are, in my opinion, truly unexplainable. The first, about a horse, is contributed by Brenda Livengood of Vandergrift, Pennsylvania:

My sisters and I refer to this incident as "the miracle," and I still feel amazement when I think about it.

Several years ago, my family moved to a small housing plan on the site of a former farm. We could hear noises coming from a barn on the property, but were not allowed to go near it.

One day, we saw eyes looking through a small window. We investigated and found six horses and ponies, all in pathetic shape. We convinced the owner of the barn, who came by only once a week to care for the animals, to sell them to us for five dollars apiece.

Nag, a small black mare, was three years old at the time. She'd been born in the barn and had never seen sunlight or tasted grass. She was extremely vicious, and we weren't allowed near her unless accompanied by an adult.

The stall in which she'd been cooped up all her life was in the back of the main section of the barn. It was a large box stall and had a huge, heavy gate which was five feet high, six feet wide, and four inches thick. The day we let her out, it took two adults and three teenagers to move the gate. The hinges had rusted away long ago. It had to be picked up to be moved. Even with five of us lifting, we left deep drag marks in the dirt. We left the gate leaning against the wall about ten feet from its opening. We had to get it out of the way while we removed tons of manure from the stall.

After we fenced pastures for the horses, we just let Nag follow the other horses. She would make an effort to hurt you if you were in her fields. Over the months we had tried roping her, crowding her with other horses, and leaving her feed where she'd have to see us, but nothing worked.

One February morning, I went to the barn to feed the horses and noticed Nag was in the far end of the field, lying under a tree. I ran toward her thinking she was hurt, but when she saw me she jumped up and began chasing me. Nag couldn't catch me, for the snow was deep and she'd had a foal the night before. The foal was shivering badly and fell every few steps. Nag kept stopping to wait for it.

I returned to the safety of the barn and saw that the foal was taking longer and longer to get up. I knew it would die if I couldn't get it warm, fed, and vetted, but the mare wouldn't let me within fifty feet of her. As I ran back to the house to get help, I saw Nag standing over the foal, who no longer attempted to stand.

I was gone only five minutes, and returned with my two sisters, my mom, and our neighbor, who was visiting. We found Nag and her baby in the back stall eating hay. And the gate was closed. The gate was settled exactly into place. There were no drag marks in the dirt, as there were the day we moved it.

Both horses were dry and seemed healthy. Nag nickered when we came in, making no attempt to shatter the wood to get at us. Nag, who had never been touched by any of us, let our neighbor tend to her baby. She has been tolerant, if not friendly, toward humans from that time on.

Our boots had tracked snow into the barn, but there were no tracks from the horses. Their tracks came up from the field and then disappeared. I know this sounds hard to believe, but it happened.

One more thing: When talking to the owner of the barn, I learned that a work horse had died in that same stall many years before while foaling. Her foal, a red-and-white pinto, also died. Nag's foal was a red-and-white pinto! He's a healthy show horse today.

Marilyn Harper*, a psycho-therapist from New York, had her heart set on acquiring a black dog. After a six-month search, she found a litter of eight-week-old, Lab-shepherd puppies which contained both black and yellow pups at a local humane society.

Each time Marilyn reached for any of the black puppies, however, a little yellow female snapped and pushed them away and jumped into Marilyn's hands. The yellow pup seemed to know she should be chosen for this particular human.

And time has proven her right. The puppy was Belinda, and she and Marilyn have been together for nearly sixteen years. "It's been a special and very psychic relationship," Marilyn says.

An example of this involves one of Marilyn's clients, a woman who suffered great pain from a chronic, genetic deterioration of her hips. This woman was referred to Marilyn by a doctor who prescribed "body therapy" for her, in hopes of making her life more comfortable.

Body therapy involves sensory awareness. The client lies on a table as the therapist works with him or her to discover tension points in the body; tension worsens pain, and awareness of tension spots can result in less pain.

The woman came for her first treatment. Marilyn routinely shut Belinda, then age nine, in her upstairs bed-

---

* Name changed to assure client's privacy.

room while she worked with clients downstairs. The spot on which Belinda invariably laid was directly over the table used in treatment.

That day, when the woman arose from the table after treatment, her pain was completely gone. The physical condition remained, but there was simply no more pain. Both she and Marilyn were amazed, delighted, and puzzled.

After the ecstatic woman left, Marilyn went upstairs to let Belinda out of the bedroom. To her horror, Belinda dragged herself, trembling and crying, across the floor. The beautiful dog's hips were paralyzed. They were completely frozen.

Marilyn held and soothed Belinda until she fell asleep in her arms. When Belinda awoke, about an hour and a half later, she was fine. Neither Belinda nor the client were troubled by painful hips again.

PART TWO
Altruistic Animals

"HIS APOLOGIES"
1932

by Rudyard Kipling

Master, this is Thy Servant. He is rising eight weeks old.
He is mainly Head and Tummy. His legs are uncontrolled.
But Thou hast forgiven his ugliness, and settled him on Thy
    knee . . .
Art Thou content with Thy Servant? He is *very* comfy with
    Thee.

Master, behold a Sinner! He hath committed a wrong.
He hath defiled Thy Premises through being kept in too long.
Wherefore his nose has been rubbed in the dirt, and his self-
    respect has been bruisèd.
Master, pardon Thy Sinner, and see he is properly loosèd.

Master—again Thy Sinner! This that was once Thy Shoe,
He has found and taken and carried aside, as fitting matter to
    chew.
Now there is neither blacking nor tongue, and the Housemaid
    has us in tow.
Master, remember Thy Servant is young, and tell her to let
    him go!

Master, extol Thy Servant, he has met a most Worthy Foe!
There has been fighting all over the Shop—and into the Shop
    also!
Till cruel umbrellas parted the strife (or I might have been
    choking him yet),
But Thy Servant has had the Time of his Life—and now shall
    we call on the vet?

Master, behold Thy Servant! Strange children came to play,
And because they fought to caress him, Thy Servant wentedst
    away.
But now that the Little Beasts have gone, he has returned to
    see
(Brushed—with his Sunday collar on) what they left over
    from tea.

Master, pity Thy Servant! He is deaf and three parts blind.
He cannot catch Thy Commandments. He cannot read Thy
    Mind.
Oh, leave him not to his loneliness; nor make him that kit-
    ten's scorn.
He hath none other God than Thee since the year that he was
    born.

Lord, look down on Thy Servant! Bad things have come to
    pass.
There is no heat in the midday sun, nor health in the wayside
    grass.
His bones are full of an old disease—his torments run and in-
    crease.
Lord, make haste with Thy Lightnings and grant him a quick
    release!

Chapter 7

Heroic Dogs

They say that the first inclination which
an animal has is to protect itself.
—Diogenes Laertius

When Kay Wilcox lived in Colorado, she had a black Labrador retriever named Duchess. The cellar of the home in which Kay lived at that time was an old, dirt dugout type where Kay stored fruit.

One day when Kay went down to get some fruit, Duchess insisted on going with her. The dog was highly agitated and attempted several times to push Kay away from one corner of the dark cellar, which was where Kay wanted to go.

Finally, Duchess stuck her head down in the spot she'd been warning Kay about and was bitten in the face by a large rattlesnake.

"We doctored her immediately," Kay says. "Her whole body became horribly swollen, and after the swelling left she was in real poor shape for a while. But she did live through it."

Contrary to the quotation at the beginning of the chapter, the stories sent to me indicate there are plenty of altruistic pets out there. Altruism is the act of saving or helping others, while putting oneself at risk in the process. Relatively few humans have the courage to do this, although nonhuman animals often perform heroic acts. There is nothing more moving than a small animal trying to protect its human from a big danger.

There is an ancient tale from India that claims a serpent ate Adam and Eve the first two times God made them. Then God tried once more, this time creating a dog to protect Adam and Eve. The dog's barking kept the serpent away.[1]

From the tiny Chihuahua to the huge mastiff, all dogs are said to be descended from the wolf. It is probably the highly-socialized aspects of the wolf pack that have made dogs such ideal companions for humans.

Dogs have helped humans in every area of life during the past ten thousand years (give or take two millennia). They have hunted with and for us, guarded us from harm, herded livestock, transported us by pulling sleds, rescued avalanche and earthquake victims, fought alongside us in battle, tracked down criminals, guided the blind, sniffed out drugs and bombs, and, in addition to all the rest, offered us unconditional love.

The hardened war veteran Napoleon Bonaparte was once moved to tears on a battlefield by the sight of a dog who, in howling confusion, tried both to protect and get help for the body of his slain master. It impressed Napoleon that although the fallen soldier must have had friends in the camp, only his dog had not abandoned him.[2]

Celia Talus Coffin, now living in Lake Shastina, California, enjoys folklore and reminiscent writing as hobbies. A native of southwest Washington, Celia says her grandparents were religious people who believed every child had a guardian angel, which is why they passed this story down to her:

Francis Whealdon was among the first settlers in the Naselle River Valley in southwestern Washington State. He acquired a farm—and a dog—in 1872. Seven years later he married Elizabeth, a teacher. They had two sons, Ray and Frank.

In this heavily-forested part of Washington, there was the never-ending job of clearing land for pastures, gardens, orchards, homes, and buildings. Frank was busy working on a new homesite one calm, sunny afternoon.

There wasn't a breath of air stirring. The trees were completely still.

Elizabeth had finished her housework and had taken their two sons, both less than four years old, across the meadow where her husband was at work. The boys raced around until they were tired and sleepy, so the parents placed them on a blanket under a large spruce tree. The old dog—a typical farm dog of mixed collie-shepherd heritage—curled up at the children's feet.

Elizabeth stood watching her husband work. They were about two hundred feet from where the little boys were lying. Suddenly, the dog sprang up growling. Then he spent several frenzied minutes tugging at the children's feet and rushing back and forth between them and the puzzled parents. The dog finally became so frantic that the parents moved the boys to see if that would quiet him.

They had scarcely put the little ones under another tree when a huge limb from the first tree crashed to the ground, completely covering the spot where the children had been lying. Had the dog's alarm been disregarded, the boys would have been killed.

Was the dog's sense of hearing so keen, he heard the limb creaking though the parents didn't? Was it ESP? Or was it the boys' guardian angels using the old dog to give warning, as Elizabeth always believed?

It probably *was* the dog's superior hearing that alerted him to the danger, but what a special dog to realize that the limb was about to crash to the ground, and to figure out he had to get the children out of its path. Why didn't he merely run to safety himself? After all, he put himself in jeopardy by staying beneath the tree to tug at the children.

How fortunate that the parents heeded the old dog's actions. In story after story the same behavior emerges when describing how animals alert humans to danger.

The description of the old dog rushing back and forth between the parents and the children is typical behavior of an animal desperately trying to communicate a problem.

When a pet displays great agitation, especially accompanied by staring at the human's face and by darting back and forth between the human and another point, it would be wise to investigate. The animal is trying with all its might to tell the human something is amiss. Taking this behavior seriously could prevent serious injury or even death to another human or animal.

It's amazing how many people misunderstand such behavior and simply wonder if something is wrong with the animal, often concluding it must have to go to the bathroom.

It is said that William of Orange, by heeding his pug's warning, averted disaster. The enemy infiltrated William's camp one night as he campaigned in the Low Countries. Only the desperate scratching of his little pug awoke him in time to react effectively, and his great affection for the breed stemmed from that incident.[3]

Even very young dogs can demonstrate loyalty and heroism. Suzette Saint-Ours, of Mendon, New York, shared seventeen years with a beautiful dog named Honey (more about Honey in Chapter Fourteen).

Back when Honey was young, people didn't routinely spay and neuter their pets, and Honey had a litter of pups when she was only a year old. She was too young to be a good mother, refusing to break the sacs or nurse the puppies, and Suzette ended up raising them for her.

Except for one pup named Pandy (Pandora), all the pups had found homes by the time they were eight weeks old. By then it was winter. One day Honey and her daughter Pandy were outside playing in the snow in a fenced-in yard which contained a swimming pool.

Suddenly Pandy was at the back door, barking with an urgency that would not be denied. She wouldn't stop until Suzette went out. Pandy led her to the pool and up the ladder to the deep end. Honey was in the pool, hanging to the edge by her claws; she'd broken through the ice, and her back end was completely submerged under it. Suzette managed to pull her out. Her hindquarters were almost frozen, and she was stiff for three days afterward.

The puppy saved her mother's life, even though the mother would have let Pandy die at birth without Suzette's intervention. Recognizing that Honey was in danger and perceiving that the only way to help her was to seek human assistance seems particularly amazing in view of the fact that Pandy was only eight weeks old at the time. Her action would be the equivalent of a human one-year-old infant getting help for a drowning adult.

Another story about a remarkably capable dog is written by Carol Strader of Middle Grove, New York:

In 1979, a girl gave me a black-and-tan German shepherd named Zack. He was two years old. A year later, Zack saved a man from drowning.

We were living in Georgia at the time, and folks used to gather at a man-made pond in the area to swim and picnic. One Saturday afternoon, I took Zack and my daughter Fran to this pond for the afternoon. A man who was obviously mentally retarded wandered to the edge of the pond and watched the people in the water swimming and playing. Zack was in the back of the truck, and we were there with him.

I saw the man walk down the bank into the water. He lay in the water on his stomach, with his feet out behind him and his arms out in front of him, as if to swim. He managed to get out into waist-deep water. He didn't understand that he could stand up; he panicked, arms still outstretched and face bobbing in and out of the water.

I yelled to some boys out in the water to help the man. They just watched and kept telling him to stand up, not realizing he didn't understand.

When I yelled, Zack jumped from the back of the truck and ran to the floundering man. Zack grabbed his shirt and started pulling him back to the bank of the pond.

When the man's knees touched the pond bottom, he stood up. He was okay, except for his shirt where Zack had torn it as he pulled him in. It all happened very fast.

Zack was a hero, but that's not all that happened that day. Later in the afternoon, a man came to the pond, got out of his pickup truck, set up a target, and shot at it with a pistol. Zack leaped from the back of my pickup again and ran full speed toward the man with the gun.

The man saw Zack charging straight at him and pointed the pistol at my dog. I was running behind Zack, desperately yelling, "Don't shoot him! Don't shoot him!"

Zack tore up to the man and took the pistol right out of his hand. Then he simply stood there with the gun in his mouth.

The man said, "I thought he was going to attack me. I was going to shoot him." I thanked the man for not shooting Zack, gave him his pistol back, and we went home!

Kris Crance, of Clyde, New York, came home from work one night to find her dogs missing and their chains broken. Her dogs were Rebel, a Dalmatian (mentioned in Chapter One), and Muffy, a small Peek-a-poo-type dog.

It was a blustery winter evening, with a snowstorm fast approaching. Kris set out to look for the dogs, walking everywhere she could think of and calling them repeatedly. She was particularly worried about Muffy, since it was obvious from the remaining chain that the little dog was dragging about three yards of chain behind her.

After half an hour of frantic searching and calling, Rebel suddenly appeared. Kris put him in the house and continued looking for Muffy but, in the howling wind, she doubted the dog could hear her. Finally, in desperation, she let Rebel out again to help search.

Rebel immediately headed for a far-off woods, so distant that Kris hadn't considered looking there. She followed and Rebel led her straight to Muffy, who was about three hundred feet into the woods, caught with her chain wrapped around a log.

"I doubt Muffy would have survived the night," Kris says. "It was bitterly cold, and I don't think I'd ever have found her by myself."

In the 1940s, Mary K. Winter, of Clyde, New York, had some neighbors who paid a hefty price for Queenie, a dog they claimed was a Canadian shepherd. The young dog often ran away from her owners to go to Mary's house to play with Mary and her younger brothers and sisters. Queenie loved children and couldn't be kept away from them. Admitting defeat, the neighbors gave Queenie to Mary.

Queenie proved to be an outstanding cattle dog. Mary's husband, Wilfred, had only to say, "Queenie, bring the cows up!" and she did the job quickly and with no fuss. After Queenie had a litter and the Winters made the decision to keep one of the pups (Chapter Eleven), they gave Queenie to a local cattle dealer, who was delighted to get her.

When Queenie had been with this man for a number of years, Mary paid her a visit. She found the dog healthy and happy and could see that she was highly valued by her new owner.

"You know, I wouldn't take a million dollars for that dog," said the cattle dealer. "She saved my life *twice!*"

He went on to tell Mary of two life-threatening incidents, once when a boar pig had him cornered and another terrifying day when a bull trapped him. Both times he called for Queenie, and both times she sailed over a fence and grabbed the charging beasts by their noses, diverting them so that the man could escape. Luckily, she also escaped injury.

Queenie lived to be nearly sixteen years old. When she died, she was buried under an old apple tree, with a marker on her grave. That was special treatment indeed for a farm dog of those days.

Marilyn Harper's Lab-shepherd dog Belinda (mentioned in Chapter Six) is credited with saving a woman from rape. At the time, Marilyn and Belinda were living alone across from a park. It was early Christmas morning. Marilyn, who'd been up late visiting her family on Christmas Eve, was sleeping soundly.

Around two o'clock in the morning, Marilyn thought she heard a woman crying for help. Half awake and not entirely sure she hadn't dreamt it, Marilyn got out of bed and staggered to the front door. As she opened it and turned on the front light, Belinda bolted out.

Silently, the dog streaked toward the park. Marilyn screamed for her to come back, but Belinda was quickly swallowed up by the night. A moment later, a young woman emerged from the spot where Belinda had just disappeared. She ran awkwardly to Marilyn's house, pulling up and fastening her jeans as she ran. Belinda had frightened the man off before an actual rape took place. Marilyn called the police, and Belinda eventually returned.

When Marilyn questioned the neighbors up and down her street on Christmas Day, she learned they had all heard the woman's cries for help. Not one of them had gotten up to turn on an outside light or call the police, not to mention taking direct action.

A dog can express its devotion in ways other than heroic. An historical story of a dog's touching loyalty is that of Marie Antoinette's papillon, Thisbe. It is said the little dog waited outside the prison the entire time Marie Antoinette was confined prior to her execution.[4]

A Native American Indian story claims that when life on earth comes to an end, a worthy man will awake in the next world to discover the spirit of his loyal dog, eager to escort him forever. Wouldn't it be nice to spend all eternity with dogs like these?[5]

Chapter 8

Unusual—but Helpful—Relationships

The wolf also shall dwell with the lamb,
And the leopard shall lie down with the kid . . .
—Isaiah 11:6

It seems to strike humans as particularly fascinating when an animal develops a relationship with another animal that would seem to be its natural enemy. Such a story is told by Suzette Saint-Ours, a woman who devotes her life to helping animals in a variety of capacities, and her veterinarian husband, Dr. Laurel Kaddatz of Mendon, New York.

Suzette and Laurel have an eight-year-old bluetick coonhound named Taj (Quade Blue Taj). Taj, whose mother was a field champion, has no interest in hunting. Far from it—she *saves* animals.

Taj is forever bringing home uninjured, newborn wild animals—bunnies, birds, turtles and frogs—and carries them so gently they aren't even wet from her mouth. Suzette cares for them tenderly.

When Suzette isn't nurturing the helpless babies, Taj protects them. She carefully wraps herself around them and growls at any cat or other dog who dares approach.

Taj, a spayed female, dotes upon young animals of all types, with one exception—her own kind. She can't abide puppies and won't stay in the same room with one.

Ruffles is a black cocker spaniel owned by Polly and Jim Bullock, animal lovers living in Sodus, New York.

This compassionate little dog saved a kitten one night when the temperature plunged below zero.

The Bullocks had put Ruffles out to relieve himself at the usual time, letting him out through the door which leads to their deck. He immediately returned and ran up and down the stairs as if to draw their notice to something below. Once he had their attention, Ruffles stayed down at the bottom of the stairs, huddled over an object.

Jim went down to see what was up, and found Ruffles solicitously nuzzling a small, furry, frozen lump. Jim saw it was a kitten and rushed it into the house.

The Bullocks didn't believe the kitten would survive. Ice balls hung from her, all the hair on her tummy had frozen off and her tail had a sharp bend in it, as though it had been frozen through.

For the next two days, the kitten stayed under the wood stove or cuddled close to Ruffles. The cocker hovered over her, licking her frequently. Bit by bit, she began to improve.

The kitten eventually made a full recovery. Polly and Jim named her Nermal, and today she is a gorgeous, gray, long-haired Persian-type with enormous green eyes and a fluffy tail.

Ruffles and Nermal are still great friends and play nicely together. When Ruffles passes beneath her chair, Nermal sometimes puts her paw down and gently combs through his hair with her claws. But when she tries to sleep with him these days, the amount of heat radiating from her fifteen-pound body is too much for Ruffles; he begins panting and has to leave.

I had a beautiful dark palomino mare named Angel who helped save a dog. It was surprising, because she disliked dogs. In fact, she didn't like people.

I bought her when I lived in Colorado. Angel had been pulled in off the range, "rough broke" and treated pretty harshly in her time. I couldn't blame her for not having a love of humans.

I bred her to a good Arabian stallion and brought her East with me when I moved. She didn't adjust well to living in a pasture with thirty other horses at her new home, which was the only accommodation I could find, or afford, at the time. (Horses have to establish a pecking order with each new arrival.) Angel lost a great deal of weight and received so many injuries from the hazing that I began to fear for the foal she was carrying.

After much searching, I found a woman named Gloria who was experienced with horses and was willing to board Angel at her place. She took excellent care of the mare and gave her the pampering she badly needed at that point.

Gloria adored her dog, Jack. But something was wrong with him; he seemed to have been born without sense, and was kept chained at all times to prevent doing injury to himself or others.

Angel had a spacious stall at Gloria's, with a lovely paddock adjoining it. Angel was in this paddock one day while Gloria was cleaning her stall. Suddenly, Angel ran to the window, poked her head through it, and whinnied at Gloria with some urgency. Then she ran off. The mare repeated this action twice more before Gloria responded and came out to investigate.

When Gloria appeared, Angel cantered to the far end of the paddock, stopped, and stared toward a distant field. Gloria followed her gaze and saw Jack running across the field, clearly trying to get far away as quickly as he could.

Because Angel let her know in time and showed her where the dog was headed, Gloria was able to intercept and recapture Jack before he came to any harm. She always credited Angel with saving Jack's life.

It was the only caring act Angel ever performed. Her life had not been a happy one. It's my opinion that she appreciated the tender care Gloria provided, especially since it resulted in her having a stronger, healthier foal. I believe helping to save Jack was Angel's way of thanking Gloria.

Belinda, the Lab-shepherd cross belonging to Marilyn Harper, once helped a kitten out of a jam, even though she wasn't particularly fond of the young feline.

At that time, Marilyn and Belinda were sharing a house with a roommate, who had a tiny gray tiger kitten. All kittens are naughty and wildly playful, of course, but this particular youngster was continually getting herself into serious predicaments.

Although Belinda is, according to Marilyn, "basically empathetic to everything living," she appeared to have no special relationship with the dynamic kitten. In fact, Marilyn noticed, Belinda seemed to watch with puzzled amazement as the kitten got away with breaking every household rule Belinda respected.

One afternoon when Marilyn arrived home from the university she attended, Belinda met her at the door and displayed much more than her usual loving greeting. The dog was upset and bursting with urgency. Staring at Marilyn's face, she ran back and forth between Marilyn and the back of the house, indicating she should follow her.

Marilyn's normal routine upon arriving home was to go upstairs, change her clothes, and relax; she wouldn't have gone to the back of the house for any reason at that time of day. But Belinda made it clear that she must come. Marilyn flung her books down, and Belinda led her through the house to the back door.

There was the kitten, caught by one tiny front claw hooked into the door chain, dangling helplessly and silently. There was no support for any part of the kitten's body, and no way of telling how long she'd been there. Luckily, the kitten seemed unharmed after her ordeal, but if Belinda hadn't led Marilyn to her she might have remained there for hours longer.

Sometimes animals of different species will form a conspiracy of sorts. Such was the case with my white-whiskered black cat, Slick, and my Australian shepherd, Cowgirl.

Cowgirl had a variety of health problems in her later years and took steroids, among other medications, for a long time. As a result, she was perpetually hungry. Her main obsession was dog biscuits.

When these partners in crime first began "the dog biscuit caper," I was keeping the treats in one of my bottom kitchen cupboards. Cowgirl couldn't open a cupboard door, but Slick could.

Cowgirl would wait by the cupboard while Slick obligingly clawed it open, enabling the dog to stick her head in the box and gulp down as many biscuits as she could before I came to investigate the suspicious sounds of gluttony. It was difficult for Cowgirl to pretend innocence, since her head was often stuck in the box when I barged into the kitchen.

To counteract this, I began keeping the treats on top of the kitchen counter, which Cowgirl couldn't reach. I should have known those two would soon work out a new system. Cowgirl had only to stand by the counter and look longingly up at the biscuits; Slick would jump on the counter, knock the box over, pry open the top, and bat them, one by one, down to his waiting friend.

We finally put child-proof locks on the cupboard doors which, luckily for Cowgirl's waistline, were also cat-proof.

Ruth A. Rudd, an artist from Bradenton, Florida, writes of another "unnatural" relationship, this time between a dog and a wild toad:

We had a wonderful dog named Laddie, part shepherd and part collie. I fed him pellet dog food out in the carport every evening around six o'clock. One evening a toad came to eat the pellets. The dog didn't like the idea too well, but I said, "Laddie, the toad needs to eat too. Let him eat with you."

That dog seemed to know and understand what was said to him as well as a human. So after that they ate together. But how did that toad know when I would bring the pellets to put in the dog dish? He was there every evening at the same time. Otherwise I never saw him.

This story is hard to explain, not so much because of the cooperation of the dog (amazing enough), but

because it's believed toads won't eat anything that does-
n't move. Toads are, however, considered the most intelligent of the amphibians—maybe it was smart enough to
save itself some work.[1]

Georgia Bender, of Kittanning, Pennsylvania, once
had a cat who went against his nature because she asked
him to. Georgia writes:

> Sputty (mentioned in Chapter Five) was a tough old
> tom cat, and he was a terror to birds. He ravaged blue
> jay nests so frequently that the jays dived on him at ev-
> ery opportunity and pecked him severely. Sleep was
> regularly broken on a summer dawn by the noisy accu-
> sations of jays as Sputty strolled through the back yard.
>
> Then a friend gave my husband two parakeets in a cage.
> He carried the cage into the house, set it on the dining
> room table and the family gathered to watch the birds.
> The cats (who were so much a part of the family that
> mentioning them separately seems redundant) gathered
> too, in our laps, with Sputty in mine.
>
> His eyes widened, then narrowed. His body tensed and
> he crouched lower, lower, until he barely peeped over
> the edge of the table. He might as well have had a neon
> sign over his head flashing LUNCH.
>
> I rapped him lightly between the ears and said calmly,
> "No."
>
> He turned and looked at me.
>
> "These are mine."
>
> Sputty relaxed and *never* attempted to attack the para-
> keets. A few times, however, when he was annoyed with
> me, he went over to the cage, looked about to be sure I
> was watching, and whipped his paw back and forth
> across the bars, driving the birds into a screeching
> frenzy.

Fahe Yarbrough, of Sarasota, Florida, tells the story
of two of her pets, a male collie named Sandy (Sandy
Gandson) and a cat they called John L. Sullivan, both

sable-and-white in color. These two animals lived together for many years and developed an amusing daily ritual.

When Fahe and her husband Peter (Dr. O.D. Yarbrough) lived on a farm in Virginia, Peter went down to the barn first thing every morning. And each morning he was followed by Sandy the dog, who in turn was followed by John L.

Along the path of this daily mini-parade was a pile of sand and a pile of gravel—the Yarbroughs were always making cement for one purpose or another. Invariably, Sandy paused to cock a leg on the pile of sand, and then went on his way.

Daily, says Fahe, John L. Sullivan peered around in shame and horror to make sure there were no witnesses to such appalling bad manners. Then he carefully scooped sand over the spot on which his friend had urinated, obviously embarrassed that Sandy's mother had never taught him better etiquette and anxious to conceal the evidence.

In two of the stories in this chapter, Laddie the dog and Sputty the cat were ordered not to hurt certain other animals (the toad and the parakeets). Surprisingly, Laddie and Sputty appeared to understand and respect this edict.

Even more surprising (delightfully so) is that the pets in the rest of the stories *voluntarily* befriended and helped animals of other species. Perhaps the day is fast approaching when the leopard really will lie down with the kid.

Chapter 9

Heroic Cats

If a man could be crossed with the cat, it would improve man, but it would deteriorate the cat.
—Mark Twain

Dogs, of course, are known for their loyalty and protectiveness, while throughout history cats have been considered helpful chiefly because of their use in rodent control. An exception to this is the Siamese who, owned by the King of Siam, supposedly guarded the palace against unwanted intruders.[1]

Legend has it that cats were created by a need to kill the mice rampantly breeding and overrunning Noah's Ark, causing great loss of the food stored on board to feed the other animals. The story goes that the lioness sneezed forth a cat when Noah asked for help, and the cat soon took care of the rodent problem.

Ancient Chinese tales abound with stories of cats, both real and magical, whose cleverness at killing rats and mice result in riches for their lucky owners. In one such story, a poor scholar spends his last money to buy a cat painted on a silk scroll after he has seen her jump from the scroll and kill mice in the store. He carries the scroll back to China where, lo and behold, the Imperial Palace is desperately seeking help to rid the palace of swarms of mice. The cat springs from the scroll and kills them all, and great wealth is awarded her master in gratitude.[2]

In the United States, in the late 1940s, a Cats-for-Europe Campaign was formed to protect the large amounts of food we sent overseas from being destroyed by rodents. Thousands of homeless American cats were flown to the war zone to offer their special talents.[3]

But cats can be of great help to humans in ways that have nothing to do with rat catching. Cats, in fact, are often heroic.

The famous French writer Colette was noted for her sensitive descriptions of animals, and she particularly loved cats. In "The Long Cat," Colette writes of a short-haired black cat who measured over a yard long when stretched out. For this reason, he was called The Long Cat, although his name was actually Babou.

One day a tabby kitten sired by him fell into a river. The Long Cat flung himself into the rushing waters, swam to the kitten, grabbed him by the scruff of the neck, and took him safely to shore.

The kitten hadn't made a sound until he was safe, and then he yowled mightily. This woke the kitten's mother, who, unfortunately, had slept through the drama. She saw only her half-drowned kitten with the dripping Long Cat nearby, assumed the worst and never forgave The Long Cat for trying to harm her baby.

Georgia Bender, from Kittanning, Pennsylvania, tells this story of a brave little cat:

> Little Fellow was a "leftover" kitten that we kept only because nobody else wanted him. He was one of the sweetest, gentlest cats I have ever known. He got his name from his wish to keep up with the big cats, even when he had hurt his paw and hobbled after them, mewing. "Aw, the poor Little Fellow," we'd say.
>
> One day when he was less than a year old and bright with curiosity about everything, he watched me bake cookies. As I took the pan from the oven, he stood up to see better and put his paws on the hot oven door, scorching them a little. After that he was afraid of fire and hot things in general. When I went outside to burn

waste paper, he often trotted along to watch from a safe distance, sometimes sitting on top of a nearby brick barbecue.

One October day sparks from my trash fire blew into nearby dead leaves which began to burn, and I started to stamp them out with my feet. Suddenly Little Fellow was there in the burning leaves beside me, repeatedly throwing his weight against my legs.

Some people might discount the significance of this, for I was never in any real danger, but Little Fellow must have thought I was. I think he came along to watch and protect me, just in case. And, considering his fear of fire, I found it a gesture of truly heroic devotion, one that few people could match.

Sylvia Albrecht, of Newark, New York, has a part-Siamese senior citizen named Tippy, who never hesitated when she thought Sylvia was in danger.

When Sylvia and Tippy lived in Texas, there was a German shepherd in a nearby apartment who had killed several cats belonging to other tenants.

One day when Tippy was outside, Sylvia happened to look out the screen door and saw the shepherd, belly to the ground, stalking Tippy. Sylvia raced out, grabbed her cat and, opening the screen door, pushed her into the apartment. Then she turned to confront the dog, hollering at him to go away. When the shepherd was about three feet away, he jumped Sylvia, grazing her knee with his mouth.

When she'd shoved Tippy into the apartment, Sylvia thought she'd shut the door, but it hadn't latched. In the commotion of her hollering and the dog attacking, she realized Tippy had run out and was by her side, back arched, hissing and spitting at the huge dog. This distracted the shepherd enough for Sylvia to scoop Tippy up and flee back to the safety of the apartment.

Tippy came to Sylvia's rescue again a few years later when they were living in upstate New York. They were out in the garden with one of Sylvia's dogs, Ted, a shepherd-golden retriever cross. Ted was being harassed by deer flies; he snapped loudly at one of the pesky insects, accidentally bumping Sylvia in the process. She yelled at Ted to be careful.

Tippy flew into action and chased Ted around and around the garden. Hearing teeth snap, bodies meet, and Sylvia's yelp had convinced Tippy her human needed help once again.

When tested, cats prove highly intelligent, able even to solve series of related problems. Feral cats captured for testing appear to learn considerably faster than cats who have been reared in cages, indicating that a variety of experiences results in a sharper mind.[4] Perhaps this quicker intelligence also results from having to depend only on themselves to survive.

Our pet cats fall somewhere in between, neither feral nor cage-reared, and we have ample proof of their intelligence in our daily lives. But once in a while a *very* special cat comes along . . . a cat, for instance, like Mons.

Linda Youngman, a cat lover and breeder of Turkish Angoras from Sodus, New York, had the privilege of owning Mons. A short-haired, black-and-white "tuxedo-suited" cat, Mons was originally named Monster because, says Linda, "He was a terror in his younger days!" Mons was a highly valued member of the family even before the night he transformed himself into both hero and bloodhound.

On this particular night Mons awakened Linda, who is a very sound sleeper, by marching all twenty pounds of himself over her sleeping form. Besides walking on her to rouse her, Mons meowed and licked her eyelids. When he finally succeeded in waking her, Linda heard someone trying to break into her house through the cellar door.

She grabbed a bathrobe and hurried over to a neighbor's house, where she called the police, and didn't return home until they arrived. When Linda and the police went to her house, they found the front door open and Mons sitting on the front step.

During their investigation, the police found the casing of the cellar door *and* the casing of her locked bedroom door had been ripped out. Linda was lucky to have escaped when she did—thanks to Mons.

But Mons's work wasn't done that night. He followed Linda and the police everywhere, rubbed against their legs and meowed continually. When Linda picked him up to quiet him, he struggled to get free, which was unlike him. Mons then ran back and forth between the humans and the front door.

Finally, they understood and followed him. Mons led them to a ditch which lay alongside the railroad tracks about a hundred feet from Linda's home. Lying in the ditch, hiding, was the man who had broken into Linda's house. The police arrested him.

After that night, whenever Mons heard a siren, he ran to Linda to alert her. He seemed to want to make her aware that trouble was afoot again, and they'd better be prepared.

Mons died two years ago at age sixteen. Losing this remarkable cat hit Linda hard, but his memory will live on; Linda has dedicated her cattery to him—it's called "Formons."

Karen Strossman, a dedicated lover of animals from Rose, New York, also had a cat who alerted her to danger by walking on her as she slept. At that time, Karen was living in an apartment in Louisville, Kentucky, and the cat, a striking long-haired yellow tabby, was named Katie.

When this incident occurred, Karen had one baby and was pregnant with another. One winter day she was sterilizing rubber baby bottle nipples in a pan of boiling water. She left the kitchen and went to check on the baby, who was sleeping peacefully. Karen then lay down on her own bed, intending to rest for just a few moments. She fell fast asleep.

While Karen slept the water in the pan boiled away. The rubber nipples began to burn, filling the apartment with foul-smelling smoke. Karen slept on.

Katie came to the rescue. Karen was sleeping so soundly that Katie literally had to walk on her face to rouse her. Karen awoke to find a cat on her face and her home filled with smoke. Groggily, she ran to the kitchen and pulled the pan off the burner.

Just then came a pounding on the door. Still half asleep and choking from smoke, Karen opened the door to find the tenant from the next apartment.

"What's wrong?" he asked, alarmed because he'd smelled the smoke.

"I burned my nipples!" Karen blurted.

The neighbor was a shy man. His gaze nervously dropped to Karen's chest. "Oh, my . . . excuse me!" he mumbled, and walked quickly away.

It's interesting that the cats involved in these stories had to get physical in order to get their humans' attention. Because cats are very small animals, and because they are often talkative even when nothing much is going on, they can easily be overlooked when they try to alert us to something amiss. Their actions must of necessity be extreme in order to gain our notice. How fortunate that our cats care enough to persevere.

Chapter 10

Heroic Horses

The horse is God's gift to man.
—Arabian proverb

I first became aware of the heroic possibilities of horses when, at age eight, I read Anna Sewell's *Black Beauty*. I sighed with admiration as Black Beauty came to the bridge that stormy night and knew something was wrong at the first contact of hooves on planks. He stopped and would not be budged. It turned out, of course, that the bridge was broken in the middle and had washed away, and Squire Gordon praised Black Beauty for saving their lives. What a horse!

But *Black Beauty* is fiction. Do such things happen in real life?

Yes, they do. What follows is the story of an extraordinary horse named Dreamy. This story was sent to me several years ago by a young girl named Dena Stickley, now living in Lancaster, South Carolina:

We have a horse named Dreamy. She's a black standardbred mare, about fifteen hands high. Dreamy is a pacer, and we got her from my grandmother after the horse was outlawed from several county race tracks because the officials believed she was unmanageable. My parents didn't agree; my father races pacing horses and my mother helps him.

Before I was born, and when my mother was eight

months pregnant with my older brother, Mom was outside cutting down small saplings for firewood, because
my father was working two jobs at the time. My mother
is a very hardy woman.

Because of her pregnancy, she had to lie on the ground
to cut down the trees. When she finished with the first
tree, she pulled it over to the side of our house trailer.
Then she lay down again, cut another tree, and dragged
it over to the trailer, too.

Dreamy, who was also pregnant, was watching all this
time. When my mother finished cutting down the third
tree, Dreamy trotted over, grabbed the sapling with her
teeth, and dragged it over to the pile beside the house
trailer. Dreamy took every tree Mom cut down after
that and pulled it over to the pile.

We still have Dreamy. She's twenty-six years old now. I
love her very much, and thank her every day with a car-
rot for helping my mother.

This is an amazing story, and by rights should be in
the Intelligent Animals section of the book. Long after
Dena sent this story, however, I received a letter from
her mother, D. Lynne Stickley:

Can I tell you a little more of Dreamy? Her registered
name was Bessie Sue's Dream, and she was a coal-black
mare with the longest, fullest tail I've ever seen.

My husband's mother bred and raised her, and another
member of the family broke and trained her as a two-
year-old. She had so much speed he couldn't handle
her—she became "speed crazy" and was turned out.

We bought her back when she was three, and what a
mess she was! She was more whirlwind than horse.
Going on a race track was impossible, so the dirt road
around the fairgrounds became our jogging track.

She walked constantly in her stall, as if slowing down
was impossible. We bought a nanny goat and put it with

her. That did the trick; she had found a friend, and her attitude changed.

She was always a loving mare, never mean. She never kicked or tried to hurt you. When we left her stall, she would take my coat sleeve in her mouth and hold on, as if saying it wasn't time to go.

We took her, goat and all, to the county fair race tracks. What a sight we were. The first four of our eight children were then three, four, five, and six. That made four kids, two parents, a horse, and a goat!

We had so much fun. Dreamy was not a world beater; her lungs had been damaged somewhat at age two—what we call "wind broken." But she was always there.

One day we raced at Upper Sandusky, Ohio. She was doing fine when, in front of the grandstand, our sulky broke. The impact shot my husband and the sulky straight up and over her head. Dreamy stumbled but somehow stepped over him and then she turned a full somersault. By then the rest of the horses were past and coming back around the track for the finish line. My husband and hundreds of pieces of broken sulky lay in the track.

When a horse falls, it's normal for it to panic and run, but not Dreamy. She returned to my husband and stood in front of him like a statue until the other horses had slowed down and passed. The announcer remarked about this. After all that, we borrowed a sulky from a friend and raced the second heat, finishing second by a head.

Dreamy raced several more years, but her breathing was getting worse so we retired her to the broodmare ranks. In a way we were both retired; my fifth child was on the way. This was at the point in time when Dena's story took place.

She seemed to know when I was "in foal" too. Dreamy would nuzzle and smell my growing tummy, resting her forehead against me. We shared three years of waiting for motherhood.

Then my husband was severely injured in a racing accident and could not drive for some time. Much to our dismay, we had to sell our horses and move to town. My husband took a factory job, but things weren't too bad.

After many tears, we sold Dreamy to someone who promised to love her and let her live out her days in comfort. We visited her whenever we could, but after moving to South Carolina these visits weren't often.

I wish our story had a happy ending of knee-high blue grass and endless summers, but it doesn't. When we returned home at Christmas, we found Dreamy had been destroyed, along with another mare deemed too old for service.

My heart breaks a little every time I think of it. It was so unfair and needless.

Once again (as with Black Beauty), I say "What a horse!" But this time the horse was real, and unfortunately this time there was no happy ending to the story.

Another special standardbred was Sleepy Tom. He was a famous pacer who won many races in the course of his career, even though he was completely blind. In one race, his sulky was involved in a collision, and the driver thrown out. Sleepy Tom stopped and waited for the driver to climb back into the sulky.[1]

Robert E. Lee, the great Civil War general, and his horse, Traveller, had a special relationship that spanned eight years of war and peace. The (appropriately) confederate gray horse with black mane and tail was originally called Greenbrier, but his superior endurance when traveling resulted in his being called Traveller.[2]

Traveller has been credited with saving Lee's life, either by luck or intuition. During one battle, Traveller began rearing as shells exploded around him. Lee calmed the horse, but then Traveller suddenly reared up one more time. At that instant, a round shot passed beneath the horse's belly. Had Traveller not reared at that precise moment, it's believed General Lee would have been killed.[3]

Cathy Strong Blodgett, a farmer/secretary from Lima, New York, had a part-quarter horse gelding named Hickory. One day Cathy glanced out the window of her farmhouse to see Hickory going crazy in the pasture. The chunky, liver-chestnut horse was frantically pacing beside the fence and wouldn't allow any other of the nine horses he shared the pasture with to go near the fence line. If any tried, he wheeled and chased them back, whinnying and nipping at them.

Since this was atypical behavior for Hickory, who was normally submissive to the other horses, Cathy knew something was wrong. She stayed in the house with her two babies and continued to watch through the windows.

Finally, she spotted the cause of Hickory's consternation. The pasture fence line ran alongside the driveway, and up the driveway, in broad daylight, came a skunk. "It was weaving as it walked and just acted funny," Cathy says. "It was staggering like it was drunk."

The skunk passed the horses, and then walked around the house. By the time it had completed its uneven circle of the dwelling, all the horses were out of sight. Hickory had driven the others behind the barn and made them stay there.

Any time a normally nocturnal (active at night) animal, such as a skunk, makes a daytime appearance and acts erratically, great caution should be exercised. Chances are the animal is either sick or injured. The illness might be any number of things (skunks can get both canine and feline distemper, or it might have ingested something toxic), but it could also be rabies.

If the skunk at Cathy's farm had been rabid, not only would she and her children have been in danger, but the livestock, too. Rabid skunks have been known to nip and infect pastured cows and horses. Cathy is grateful Hickory warned her, and that he kept the other horses far away from the skunk.

As these stories demonstrate, horses are particularly

sensitive animals, probably because they were prey animals throughout their evolution and had to be highly alert to their surroundings in order to survive.

With the horse's size, strength, speed, and intelligence, it's lucky for us that it took so amenably to domestication. Beyond domestication, however, the horse has proven over and over again that it can be a loyal and protective friend to humans.

Chapter 11

Other Ways of Helping

Sleeping with a cat brings good luck.
—Animal superstition

When the Wind Blew, is a children's classic written by the late Margaret Wise Brown. In the story, an old woman lives in a little house by the ocean with seventeen cats and one small blue-gray kitten. One stormy night, the old woman gets a terrible toothache and takes to her bed, feeling miserable. The little blue-gray kitten climbs in bed with her and lies against her throbbing cheek, until the pain is gone and the woman sleeps.

Our pets don't have to be heroes or specially trained to be of great help to us; they *instinctively* are. It's amazing how animals perceive when we are sad or ill and what lengths they'll go to cheer or comfort us.

This unique ability is graphically illustrated in the following story contributed by Jeanne Huenefeld of Cincinnati, Ohio:

If you ever want a doctor to look at you quickly tell him or her you have chest pains. I really did. The pain was frightening because of its location. But not only that, it extended down to the groin.

After undergoing all sorts of tests, I was diagnosed as having acute pancreatitis and was put on medication. The chest pains stopped, but there was that occasional pain in the groin that could last for a whole day, sometimes two.

Unfortunately, one of those painful episodes occurred on a day when my husband and I were to go out to dinner with some very special friends. I didn't want to cancel out, but there I was, barely able to move. Aspirin or other pain medication didn't help.

By early afternoon I decided to just lie back in my recliner with a book and read until it was time to dress and make myself go out to dinner.

No sooner was I settled in the chair when our cat, a tortoise-shell-and-white Persian-type named Lady Jayn, jumped up on me. She positioned herself across my abdomen and leg in the exact place where the pain was so great. I didn't move; I was like a wax figure in my stillness. I put aside my book and waited to see how long she would stay there.

At this point I must tell you that Lady Jayn came to us several years ago and gave birth, unbeknown to us for many weeks, to two kittens in our attic. She was quite wild, having obviously lived on her own for some time. She would never allow you to hold her or sit on your lap as other cats often do. She had never jumped up on anyone's lap and purred herself to sleep, *never*!

But there she was. I kept hoping my husband would come into the room and see it—he wouldn't believe his eyes. I didn't dare call to him in the next room for fear of disturbing Lady Jayn. I love that cat and therefore just decided to enjoy the closeness, the gift of her presence, so unusual to her nature.

About an hour later, my husband came to see why I was being so quiet. He was amazed to see our "wild" pet comfortably asleep on me. In another half-hour Lady Jayn awakened, jumped down, and ran off, but not until she had walked up my chest and stared me straight in the eye for an unbelievabiy tense moment.

I got up—all pain gone—dressed and went out to dinner. That was one year ago, and the pain has never returned. Neither has Lady Jayn ever again jumped up in anyone's lap, nor allowed herself to be held.

Edgar Allan Poe and his wife adored their large tortoise-shell cat, Catarina. Anyone who has read Poe's "The Black Cat"—a hair-raising story about an innocent and loving cat brutally murdered by its drunken master, but who gets its revenge in the end—might find it hard to believe the author was a cat lover. But Poe was.

Catarina is said to have sat on his shoulder as he penned his macabre stories. He thought so highly of the cat that he formally introduced her to guests and, reportedly, Catarina missed Poe to such an extent when he was away on his travels that she refused to eat while he was gone.[1]

Catarina, however, is most famous for helping Poe's young wife, Virgina, as she lay dying of consumption. The couple was impoverished at the time of her death, and couldn't afford even to buy fuel to keep their cottage in Fordham warm. It is well-documented that Virginia had but two means of keeping warm on her deathbed: her husband's greatcoat and Catarina, who constantly lay on her bosom to ward off the chill. It is further said the cat gave the impression of being fully conscious of her useful role.

Another pet who provided comfort to a famous owner was Franklin Delano Roosevelt's Scottish terrier. Murray the Outlaw of Fala Hill (called Fala) was given to FDR by his cousin when Fala was eight months old. The little dog sparkled with personality and was in on everything. Fala held press interviews, attended conferences, traveled with Roosevelt, was presented cake on his birthday, had his stocking hung from the chimney at Christmas, and was altogether a charming diversion for the ill and harassed president.

Fala's most important contribution, however, was helping his great master deal with the combined stresses of physical pain, heavy responsibility, and occasional loneliness by his willingness to sit quietly by the hour on FDR's lap. Since the dog was normally highly active, it seems evident that he suppressed his nature at those times in order to help.

Another dog of great sensitivity was Flush, the beautiful, red-brown, white-breasted cocker spaniel belonging to Elizabeth Barrett Browning. An entire book (*Flush*, by Virgina Woolf) was written about this special dog and his life with the gentle poet. The dog suppressed his naturally boisterous personality to help his ailing mistress through her years of isolation in a dark room.

In Elizabeth Barrett Browning's letters, she confessed to being astounded by Flush's understanding of words, and notes with amazement how, untaught, he opened doors by their handles with his paws. He was clearly a diverting and empathetic companion during those years of loneliness. Luckily, they both obtained greater freedom and happiness when she eloped with Robert Browning.

One more instance of a dog altering its nature in order to assist its human is the story of an Italian greyhound owned by Frederick the Great of Prussia. Frederick was once surprised by a troop of Austrians who were hunting for him. He hid beneath a bridge, and his dog, though known for its noisiness, unaccountably remained silent so that they wouldn't be found.[2]

Dogs can also be of real help with children. A dog named Bob proved to be a great baby-sitter. When Mary K. Winter, of Clyde, New York, first married, she and her husband decided to breed Mary's good cattle dog Queenie (mentioned in Chapter Seven) to a shepherd-type dog. Their intention was to keep the best male offspring. This they did, and they named the pup Bob.

After Mary had a baby boy, Bob and the baby would lie together by the hour on a quilt in the front yard. If the baby crawled toward the road, Bob gently pulled him back by the seat of the pants.

Bob also helped the little boy learn how to walk. The baby would pull himself up by grabbing on to the fur of the standing dog, and Bob slowly walked alongside the child, steadying him, for however many steps he could take. When the baby plopped back down, Bob patiently stood until he was sure the child didn't want to try walking anymore and then lay down beside him again.

A true story involving the naturalist John James Audubon displays altruism in a bird. Since the story is about a mother saving her young, perhaps it merely demonstrates instinct, but it's a remarkable story nonetheless.

Audubon took a shot at a young kite (a member of the hawk family). At the sound of the gun, the mother bird, food in her claws, flew to her baby and tenderly fed it. Audubon then shot at both of them and missed again. The mother bird, not making a sound, flew above Audubon's head and then back to her young. Gently lifting her baby, she carried it to a tree about thirty yards away.

Audubon, although admitting his emotions were stirred by the mother bird's actions, killed them both with his next shot.[3]

Old literature is another fascinating source of altruistic bird lore. It was believed, for instance, that if young pelicans were killed, the mother pelican purposefully injured herself, and the sprinkling of her blood upon the dead babies brought them back to life.[4]

And ancient Greek poets thought highly of the stork. Storks, they believed, were the world's best children. When the father stork lost his feathers in old age, his offspring gathered round and covered him with their own feathers, fed him, and supported him gently as he flew.[5]

To return to real-life stories, Dorothy Lloyd, a data processing manager and animal lover from Lima, New York, grew up on a farm. When she was eleven or twelve years old, she came into possession of a newly-hatched pigeon. She carefully raised him and doctored him when, at one point, a cat injured him. The little girl and the pigeon became inseparable pals. Thinking it was a female because of its light gray and white coloring, Dorothy named the pigeon Amy, although it turned out to be a male.

Amy didn't seem to care much for flying, but he loved to go horseback riding with Dorothy, perched on the rump of her gentle black-and-white pinto, Prince. The girl and the pigeon happily mounted on the bright horse became a familiar sight on the roads and in the surrounding towns.

Amy companionably followed Dorothy to the school bus each morning, walking behind her down the driveway to see her off. One day he unaccountably flew up on the front of the bus and, when the bus began moving, was trapped against the windshield by the air flow.

Thus he was forced to ride to the next stop, which was another farm, and when the bus stopped he hopped down and went into the barn. Unfortunately, it was milking time, and the cows were black-and-white Holsteins. You can imagine the rest. Amy was probably relieved after his ordeal to see a familiar black-and-white pattern on a large animal, and it was the most natural thing in the world for him to jump up on the animal's back.

The cow went berserk and tore out the stanchion and the milking machine in her panic. The farmer was ready to kill the pigeon, but his wife recognized it as Dorothy's pet and saved the day. When Dorothy went to get him after school, Amy flew to her shoulder, and they went home.

Dorothy's story is in this section of the book because Amy, in addition to being a captivating pet, was a "guard pigeon." He was never caged, but chose to stay on the front porch of Dorothy's farmhouse.

Amy would let no one on that porch unless a member of the family was also present. He would raise a terrible ruckus, attacking and biting those who attempted to get past him to the door. Dorothy says Amy was "better than a watchdog."

Another altruistic story, this time involving a cat, comes to us from medieval days. During the War of the Roses, Sir Henry Wyatt was imprisoned by Richard III in a chilly room in the Tower of London. It is said that a stray cat slipped into the chamber and kept Sir Henry warm with its body. Not only that, the cat regularly caught pigeons and brought them to Sir Henry, who ate them. With the cat's help, the nobleman survived and eventually returned to a life of luxury.

The last story in this chapter is about a little cat named Winifred. She wasn't a hero, nor was she especially altruistic, but she made her human feel good, and that's what this section is all about.

Cathy Strong Blodgett's late father, Les Strong of Lima, New York, was an animal lover through and through. Animals sensed it and were drawn to him. Over the years, he welcomed all sorts of critters into his home.

The family chose a tiny, long-haired, gray tabby kitten from a farm litter and named it Fred. When they discovered Fred was a female, her name was quickly changed to Winifred.

Winifred adored Les Strong, and she developed a unique morning ritual to demonstrate her devotion. Every morning without fail, Winifred went into Les's room, hopped up on his bed and meowed to wake him. When he opened his eyes and looked at her, Winifred sat up on her hind legs and raised her paw to her forehead in a smart salute!

Clearly, there is no end to the ways animals help us. Utilizing instinct and ingenuity, our pets appear able to figure out ways to assist us, either by direct action or by simply being there when we need them.

Carol Strader of Middle Grove, New York, says it well: "Animals are so unselfish in their love that I sometimes think they, not man, are the highest form of animal. After all, God made them first. If we humans could learn from our animal friends, just think what a wonderful world it would be."

PART THREE
Intelligent Animals

FOUR-FEET
"THE WOMAN IN HIS LIFE"
by Rudyard Kipling

I have done mostly what most men do,
And pushed it out of my mind;
But I can't forget, if I wanted to,
Four-Feet trotting behind.

Day after day, the whole day through—
Wherever my road inclined—
Four-Feet said, "I am coming with you!"
And trotted along behind.

Now I must go by some other round,—
Which I shall never find—
Somewhere that does not carry the sound
Of Four-Feet trotting behind.

Chapter 12

Birdbrains

. . . for a bird of the air shall carry the voice, And that which hath wings shall tell the matter.
—Ecclesiastes 10:20

In *Papa Hemingway: A Personal Memoir*, by A. E. Hotchner (Random House, 1966), the author writes of a time he and Hemingway were in Paris and as they strolled past a corn vendor, Ernest turned to him and said, "You see that old fellow? Well, he had a fifty-four-year-old parrot that caught cold one day and said 'I'm going to heaven' three times over and died."

It makes you wonder, doesn't it?

Not surprisingly, there is controversy about the capacity of talking birds to understand words. Proud owners insist their birds use words intelligently. Most scientists tend to believe that's impossible, claiming that birds merely mimic what they hear.

When Carol Strader, of Middle Grove, New York, sent me the following story about her green parakeet, Petey, I became a believer. It seems obvious that, while many birds may copy human speech with no understanding of their meaning, *some* birds clearly do possess the capacity to apply correctly words to situations. Carol writes:

Our parakeet Petey amazed us. If Weezee, our cat, went near his cage, Petey would scream out "Help! Help!" We never taught him that.

We feel he knew exactly what he was saying at times. Once Eric, my husband, fed Petey for me. When he filled Petey's seed cup and placed it back in the cage, Petey said, "Oh, thank you!"

And once I was baby-sitting a little four-month-old boy, and he started crying. He wanted his mother, and nothing I did seemed to calm him. Finally Petey yelled, "Shut up!" Also, if he saw anyone smoking, he'd say "Don't smoke!" in a loud voice.

When we first moved up here, a neighbor stopped in to welcome us, and Petey said, "Want coffee?" He'd never said that before then.

Petey would look into his mirror and go on an ego trip, telling himself how pretty and wonderful he was, kiss his image, etc. Sometimes, after he'd been praising himself for quite a while, he'd look in the mirror and say, "Shut up, Petey!"

Petey loved his mate Mimi, a blue parakeet. For a full week when she first came, he fed her because she wouldn't go to the food cup by herself. He'd kiss her, making his smacking kissing sound, and say, "Oh, baby, I love you." We don't know where he got the word "baby." My husband doesn't call me that. Petey would say, "Oh, Mommy, I love you" to me. But he would only use "baby" when talking to Mimi.

It's an odd thing, but after we got Mimi he started calling himself P.P. instead of Petey, as if P.P. were more grown-up sounding. It really was funny.

We got Petey when my husband found him in a snowbank outside work one cold February day and brought him home to me. He was missing all his tail feathers, but was otherwise fine.

Petey already knew how to talk when we found him. He spoke in both male and female voices, quavery voices such as the elderly have. But he'd only say "Hi, Mildred!" and "Oh, Henry!" Evidently he belonged to an elderly couple named Mildred and Henry.

He was a smart little bird.

Fahe Yarbrough, of Sarasota, Florida, writes:

Pretty Boy, our beautiful blue parakeet, originally belonged to another Navy couple stationed with us at Pearl Harbor. They gave him to us when they were transferred. We were delighted, as he spoke more plainly than any other bird we knew.

He was a quick learner and picked up almost anything in a day or two. He loved the cocktail hour and would sit happily on the edge of anyone's glass to share a bit of cheer.* One afternoon, with Happy Hour in full swing, he flew to my husband's shoulder and said so clearly that everyone understood him, "Have a martini, you silly little bird!"

After leaving Pearl Harbor, we took him to our farm in Virginia where he met our cat, John L. Sullivan (mentioned in Chapter Eight), for the first time. We kept telling the cat not to go near Pretty Boy's cage and not to look at him or bother him in any way.

Within a few days, Pretty Boy was calling, "Come here kitty, kitty, kitty!" John L. thought that was adding insult to injury, but he never did harm Pretty Boy.

My own experience with birds is limited to a green parakeet given to me as a child. Her name was Nicki, and although she never talked, she was nonetheless an amusing and affectionate pet. We usually left the door to her cage open, and she was free to fly around the house at will.

My parents had a friend named George, who was a bit

---

*Warning: Alcohol can kill birds. Since they are very small animals, ingesting even a tiny amount of liquor, beer, or wine can result in alcohol toxicity.

of a stuffed shirt. He would come and sit by the hour, pompously discussing politics and world affairs as we stifled yawns.

George was bald-headed and wore glasses. Nicki must have been attracted to the shine of his head. One day she flew across the room, landed on top of George's head, gleefully slid down his forehead, and then stopped herself by clutching his glasses with her talons.

It was difficult for George to maintain his dignity with a parakeet hanging upside down from his glasses, staring merrily into his eyes. The poor man didn't know what to do. But needless to say, he stopped by much less often after that.

People report innumerable amusing experiences with their pet birds. Georgia Bender, for instance, writes more about the two parakeets (mentioned in Chapter Eight) her family received as a gift:

> Since the birds had each other, they never learned to talk, but just conversed all day in "Keet." I had them in the dining room where I wrote, when suddenly they turned into typewriters. They would clack-tap away like crazy. And every once in a while one of them would yell, "Ding!"

Polly Bullock, of Sodus, New York, also loves birds. She has a feeling for them and, normally, a way with them. One day she walked into a pet shop and was delighted to see a mynah bird. Confidently, Polly strolled over to the bird and said, "Helllooo!" in that strident voice birds usually respond so well to.

The mynah was silent for several moments, bobbed his head a few times, then loudly demanded, "What's *your* problem?"

Comical antics aside, if talking birds truly *understand* what they're saying and use their vocabularies appropriately, as the first few stories in this chapter would suggest, then birds are indeed capable of reasoning.

Chapter 13

Wild Birdbrains

All animals are equal, but some animals are more equal than others.
—George Orwell

Besides the pet birds that are usually considered talkers, wild birds—such as crows, magpies, jays, and starlings—saved from harm and living with humans sometimes become delightful companions and good talkers.

Arnie, the Darling Starling, written by Margarete Sigl Corbo and Diane Marie Barras (Houghton Mifflin Company, 1983), is a beautifully written, funny, and moving story of a starling saved by Ms. Corbo as a nestling. Arnie shared her life for several gratifying years, and the personality and talking talents of this bird are almost beyond belief. The book puts a whole new perspective on a bird that is usually considered a pest.

Another bird I have come to respect greatly in the course of writing this book is the pigeon. Their homing abilities, sensitivity to pending natural disasters, and versatility as pets are impressive.

As for intelligence, scientists are now comparing the brain of a pigeon to miniaturized computers. When tested, they have an amazing ability to memorize and can remember a particular picture for years. They can also select patterns of colors in sequence and can even separate unlike versions of the same object, such as different types of chairs and cats, into categories.

Polly and Jim Bullock of Sodus, New York, know how

smart pigeons are. About ten years ago, a very upset neighborhood child carried a tiny nestling to Jim to see if he could help it. Her dog had disturbed a pigeon's nest and one of the babies had fallen out. The child rescued it from the dog's mouth.

The Bullocks looked at each other in despair. It seemed impossible that such a small, frail, traumatized bird could survive. But Jim gave it his best effort. In his mouth, Jim blended a mixture of wild bird seed, oatmeal, and the seed they fed their pet cockatiel in order to make a thin enough gruel for the young pigeon to manage. He added a drop of children's liquid vitamin, and fed the bird with an eyedropper. The pigeon, now named Dufey, grew and thrived and was soon a handsome gray bird with an iridescent head.

Dufey particularly loved Jim Bullock, who had so painstakingly nurtured him as a baby. Each day when Jim pulled into the driveway after work, Dufey flew to the car, hovered over it and, as soon as Jim stepped out, landed on his shoulder to greet him.

Dufey looked exactly like a family of pigeons that regularly came to the Bullock's outdoor feeder, and they assumed he was one of theirs. They tried to get him to socialize with them, but Dufey wasn't interested. The Bullocks were his family.

Evidently, Dufey had "imprinted" to humans. Imprinting, which occurs when a bird is very young, happens quickly and is nearly irreversible. The bird hatches and immediately attaches itself to the nearest large moving object which, in the natural course of events, would be its mother.

Some people think birds aren't very bright because they will imprint to such things as wheelbarrows or balloons and follow those objects with blind trust and love. But Nature's reason for the automatic imprinting process is to ensure the safety of the young. For by attaching itself to the mother bird and following her around, it will be fed and protected. Without this system, the mother would never be able to keep track of a large number of quick, darting babies.

If the natural imprinting process goes awry, chaos reigns. Fahe Yarbrough, now living in Sarasota, Florida, once let a duck hatch eight chicken eggs. The duck was a good mother to the baby chicks, and felt it was her responsibility to teach them to swim. She took them to a small creek, but couldn't persuade them to go in. Finally, she went in the water alone. The little chicks, uncertain but desperately wanting to be with "mama," plunged in after her and drowned.

To return to Dufey, the pigeon raised by Jim and Polly Bullock, he was extremely affectionate and responsive to humans. Dufey was entirely at ease in the world of humans, even allowing the Bullock's seven-year-old daughter to cuddle him and carry him around.

Interestingly, Dufey imprinted so completely to humans that he adopted some of their manners. He always knocked on the door before entering the house. And, although he was a good flyer, he never once flew when he was inside the house, but only walked on the floor.

Outlandish examples of reasoning in wild birds appear in old literature and lore. It was said that cranes, as they rested on one foot, held a pebble in the other; if the crane began to doze off, the pebble fell from the claws of the raised foot and struck the ground, thereby snapping the crane awake to keep it alert to attack.[1]

It was also believed that wild geese carried stones in their mouths when flying over mountains. This prevented them from making a sound, and avoided attack by eagles who might otherwise hear them.[2]

These days we have abundant real examples of reasoning in wild birds. Some birds, such as killdeers, pretend to be injured in order to draw enemies away from their eggs or young. This action is called "predator distraction."

When the bird is on its eggs or raising its young and a predator (including humans) approaches, the bird clumsily flutters away from the nest as though it has a broken wing. Remaining just out of reach, it slowly leads the enemy far from the nest. A good distance away, it suddenly recovers and flies off, although never straight back to the nest—that would be too revealing.

The killdeer's actions would seem to be a normal instinct to save its young rather than an example of reasoning, except for one thing: When grazing livestock approach a killdeer's nest, the bird moves *closer* to the nest and spreads its wings in an obvious display which causes the animals to step around the nest.[3]

Horses, sheep, or cattle, being herbivores, have no desire to kill and eat the eggs or young birds. But they could unintentionally destroy them by stepping on them. The complete change of tactics used by the killdeer, depending upon what type of animal approaches the nest, demonstrates an intelligent capacity to recognize and adapt to changing circumstances.

Ostriches, the largest living birds, have the reputation of being stupid, primarily because it is believed they hide their heads in the sand when frightened (they do not do this, by the way). In fact, they are quite intelligent. In Southwest Africa, two ostriches were used to herd sheep. All by themselves, the big birds took the flock out each morning, looked after them and brought them home in the evening. They drove the sheep by pecking at their tails.

Over the years there has been much debate about a little bird called the greater honeyguide. Legend had it that this bird cruised the jungles of Africa looking for hidden bee hives. When it found the hives, it was said, the bird flew to humans or animals (usually the honey badger, or ratel) and alerted them by calling shrilly and dancing in the air. Then it led them to the hive. The human or honey badger invaded the nest and ate the honey, leaving the wax containing the bee grubs to the bird.

Two scientists recently spent three years studying the greater honeyguide. Their just-published results say this bird does indeed lead humans to bee hives. It's the only confirmed instance of a wild species cooperating with humans to find and share food.[4]

If the capacity to use tools is what separates humans from animals, we might have to redefine the theory. A number of birds are known to use tools. On the Galapagos islands, Darwin's finches select small twigs, modify their lengths if necessary, hold them in their beaks and probe cracks to spear or scrape out insects, which they then eat.

And Egyptian vultures use stones to smash ostrich eggs in order to eat the contents. Ostrich eggs are about six to seven inches long and five to six inches in diameter (by contrast, the smallest eggs—sometimes only a quarter inch long—are laid by hummingbirds). The shell of an average ostrich egg could hold between one and two dozen chicken eggs.

Some observers claim the Egyptian vultures hold the stones in their beaks and hammer at the tough-shelled egg until it breaks, while others say they toss stones at the eggs, missing much of the time but eventually succeeding in breaking them open.

Seagulls and crows have figured out how to get at the tender morsels inside hard-to-open shellfish. They carry the shellfish high above rocks or pavement and drop them, sometimes over and over again, until the shells break apart. Then they swoop down to feast. All the above tactics require problem-solving skills.

Artistic talent in birds is displayed by the bowerbirds of New Guinea and Australia. Unlike most other male birds, the male satin bowerbird is rather drab in appearance. Perhaps to compensate for the lack of color in its plumage, it builds an elaborate, beautifully decorated bower to attract females.

The bird first clears an area and builds the basic bower from twigs, mosses, and grasses. Once constructed, each bird's individual talents emerge as he begins to decorate it. There appears to be competition among the male bowerbirds to see who can devise the most stunning bower.

Other than favoring blue as the color of choice, the bowers vary in other ways. No two are alike. They range in size from two to several feet across. The decorative patterns are intricate and the birds create them with flowers, pieces of fruit, shells, and occasionally bright man-made objects such as car keys and jewelry. The bowerbirds are said to mix the paint used in decorating the walls of the bowers themselves, creating them in their mouths by combining saliva, dirt, and fruit pulp.

Once completed, the bowerbirds spend considerable time maintaining the bowers. They keep them clean and even replace the flowers when they wilt.

The female bowerbird visits and probably inspects various bowers, eventually choosing one that, for whatever reason, most appeals to her. After mating with the male of the selected bower, she leaves and lays her eggs in a rather ordinary, nest.[5] Evidently the decorated nests are for show only.

Marie Gunshannon, of Venice, Florida, contributes the following story of wild bird reasoning:

> Mary Urban, one of our neighbors here in Venice, has a daily visitor. He's a big blue heron, standing several feet tall and his bill is about ten inches long. His name is Handsome, and it's well-deserved.
>
> Almost every day he flies into Mary's back yard and stands like a statue, his bill pointed toward the kitchen door. Mary feeds him chicken necks.* She cuts the necks in three pieces and tosses them out on the grass.
>
> One day when I was visiting, Handsome arrived. He hadn't been around for a few days, so Mary had put the chicken necks in the freezer. She threw some frozen necks in front of him. Handsome picked one up, discovered it was frozen, dropped it and tried another one.

---

*There is some controversy in Florida about the well-intentioned, but possibly dangerous (to both humans and birds), practice of feeding wild herons. There is also debate about what types of food the big birds can safely be fed. Ask your local humane society or wildlife rehabilitator for information before offering food, particularly if it consists of chicken parts or deli meats.[6]

After testing several necks, he picked one up and dropped it into the warm water in the bird bath. He waited until the neck defrosted, and then he ate it. When he found this worked, he proceeded to drop the remaining necks into the bird bath.

It's easy to understand why birdwatching is gaining in popularity; the behavior and habits of wild birds are enthralling.

As a group, birds are perhaps the most versatile of all the animals. Depending on type, birds can talk, sing, predict natural disasters, perform phenomenal homing feats, memorize and separate objects, and use various tactics to save their young from harm (depending on the type of enemy). Some birds can also herd sheep, lead humans to food, use tools intelligently, decorate their homes artistically, and even deduce how to thaw food.

The more we learn about birds, the more obvious it becomes that to be called "birdbrained" is a compliment.

Chapter 14

Reasoning Dogs

There cannot be found in the animal kingdom a
bat, or any other creature, so blind in its own
range of circumstance and connection, as the
greater majority of human beings are
in the bosoms of their families.
—James Abram Garfield

Joy Watrous, an animal lover from Moravia, New York, has an eleven-year-old, female Doberman pinscher named Fritz who showed great understanding one night.

For most of her life, Fritz has wrapped herself in a blanket when she lies down to rest or sleep. According to Joy, she does a thorough job of covering herself. Fritz either lies on top of the blanket (which has a Garfield/Odie pattern) and tugs it over herself with her teeth, or crawls under it and flips it over her body. Either way, the end result is a dog whose body is neatly and completely wrapped, with only her head uncovered.

Fritz appears to use the blanket for both warmth and security. "If she's not covered by the blanket when she goes to bed at night," says Joy, "she fusses and can't sleep."

Joy's mother-in-law is a diabetic. Since poor circulation is typical in diabetics, her feet are often cold. One evening, she was visiting Joy and complained out loud about her feet being cold.

Fritz immediately stood up, went to her blanket, and brought it to the woman. The dog carefully laid the blanket over the woman's feet, and then lay down and snuggled close. Joy and her mother-in-law were astounded and very touched.

How does one explain something like that? Fritz's action seems to exhibit a genuine understanding of human words, empathy to a human condition, and a reasoning ability in figuring out a solution to a human's problem.

When we talk about the ability of animals to reason, we get into murky water. "Anthropomorphism" is the attributing of human thoughts, emotions, and motives to animals. Many animal lovers anthropomorphize their pets and, for this reason, stories about these animals are looked upon with skepticism by scientists.

This skepticism is understandable, since there's no way to repeat precisely what the animal did; the circumstances could never again be identical. Because the occasional amazing behavior of a pet in a unique situation cannot be repeated in a laboratory, these stories are considered "anecdotal."

Through living closely with humans for many thousands of years, domestic animals have picked up some of our ways and are highly attuned to our thoughts and emotions. As discussed in Part One, our pets are experts at reading our body signals and auras.

But how different are we, really, from nonhuman animals? We have many instincts in common, of course, such as nurturing and protecting our young and fleeing from danger. Our homes, with the exception of heating systems, are the same as those of animals living in the wild: Both have specific areas in which to eat, bathe, void, and store food. Animals mark their territories with scent; humans use property deeds and fences.[1]

With so much in common, it's natural that we "humanize" animals. Some believe the assumption that animals think and feel as we do is conceit on the part of the human, but what other frame of reference do we have? It's not as though our pets are alien life forms from another planet. We are all animals, after all.

How well do we humans really know one another? Even within the same family, we cannot know exactly what another person is thinking or feeling. That ignorance is multiplied if we're among foreign humans with different languages and customs.

In judging true intelligence in nonhuman animals, we have to differentiate instinct and/or training from an ability to reason. Nature has provided all animals with instincts to ensure the survival of each species, and instincts by themselves are nothing short of miraculous. But true intelligence involves more, and requires a certain amount of creative thinking.

An animal's response to a given situation is influenced by its genes, training, and life experiences—the same things which apply to the reaction of each human. Two dogs can react to the same situation with exactly opposite behavior, just as two humans might.

The best way to distinguish a reasoned action from an instinctive or learned action by our pets is to observe how they handle a situation they have never before encountered. With neither instinct nor prior experience to fall back on, the animal will have to concoct a solution from its own intelligence.

The next story tells of a dog who did just that. Ruth A. Rudd, from Bradenton, Florida, writes:

Years ago, back in the 1940s, my brother had a beagle named Butch. He thought the world of that dog, and the feeling was returned.

The dining room floor was covered with linoleum, and we had a soft rug in that room for Butch to sleep on. There was an archway between the dining room and the living room, and my brother used to sit on a couch in the living room to read the paper. Butch was not allowed in the living room, but one day, as my brother read the paper, Butch was suddenly on the couch beside him.

It was funny—how had the dog managed to cross that linoleum floor without making a sound to alert my brother? His claws should have click-clicked all the way over.

Well, my brother sent Butch back into the dining room, put the paper back up in front of his face and pretended to read it, but he was really peeking at Butch to see how he managed to sneak noiselessly across that floor.

What he saw was amazing. That dog left the rug and very slowly and carefully walked across the linoleum *on the back pads of his feet*! It was quite a feat to lean back and place each foot down so his toenails wouldn't make any noise and give him away. In his own tiptoeing way, he came to the couch and slipped up beside my brother. My brother sent Butch back to the dining room each time, and then watched him do it over and over again.

Do dogs reason? I think they do!

In "A Gentleman's Dogs," written by an anonymous nineteenth century sportsman, a greyhound named Smoaker figures out how to tell whether his master is at home. Smoaker first goes to the hallway and looks for the gentleman's hat. If it's there, the dog is content; if it isn't, Smoaker climbs the stairs to the top of the house and looks out the windows in an attempt to see where he has gone.

Animals can figure out all sorts of solutions to unique problems. A dog who found her own way of prolonging motherhood was Misty, a lovely blue merle Australian shepherd with two ghostly blue eyes. She was owned by Kay Wilcox, who now resides in Tucson, Arizona, but was living in Colorado at the time.

Misty was Cowgirl's (my Aussie's) grandmother, and that line of dogs has had a strong maternal drive. Cowgirl was a spayed female and never had pups, but she "mothered" all my other animals, cats and dogs alike. She was the dominant animal in our household, not because of age but because of temperament. She bossed everyone, kept them away from us while we ate (only *she* was allowed to beg), and physically pinned the others down to clean their eyes, ears, and genitals, and to rip burdocks from their fur.

Kay Wilcox routinely sold the many fine litters Misty produced over the years, but one year Misty rebelled. She'd had a litter of six puppies and Kay took two of them from her, when they were old enough, and sold them. Misty's reaction was to steal a pup from a beagle bitch. There lay Misty, nursing four Aussies . . . and one beagle pup.

She must still have felt a lack; after all, *two* pups had been taken from her. She made another stealthy trip and returned with two nursing kittens. Evidently that felt just right, since she stopped with them.

Kay says the sight of Misty contentedly nursing four Australian shepherd puppies, two kittens, and one beagle pup, all in a row, was something to behold.

It might have been instinct that drove Misty to replace the two pups taken from her, but think of the planning that went into getting the substitute babies. First, Misty had to locate some nursing young; then, she had to figure out how to get them away from *their* mothers.

President Warren G. Harding thought a lot of his dog, Laddie Boy. Harding saw to it that Laddie Boy ate his meals with him, had his own chair at cabinet meetings, and had his own calendar of social events. Laddie Boy even accompanied him on the golf course. The dog was so aware of everything that if Harding spoiled an approach or flubbed a simple putt while golfing, Laddie barked at him in rebuke.[2]

Carol Strader's extraordinary German shepherd, Zack (mentioned in Chapter Seven), was also uncommonly aware of humans' actions and invented his own solutions to problems. Carol writes:

I took Zack to the boat landings on the Savannah River one time. There were a lot of people there, and a little boy and girl—about three and five years old—were playing along the water's edge in ankle-deep water. Their mother was watching them.

I walked by, Zack at my side, and stopped to talk to the children's mom who remarked about what a beautiful shepherd Zack was.

The children had long, thick sticks which they were alternately throwing into the water and slapping at each other. Zack walked out and took both sticks away from them, one at a time, and put them down on the shore at my feet. I think he was afraid the children would get hurt.

Another dog who wanted to make sure children didn't get hurt was Gus, a classic, silver German shepherd. When Ed Blodgett was a boy growing up in Lima, New York, his family acquired this handsome dog, who was then two years old.

There were several youngsters in the Blodgett family, and Gus proved to be excellent with children and very protective of them. As in all large families (or small ones, for that matter), the kids became boisterous at times. On those occasions, Mrs. Blodgett would pick up a length of rubber hose and jokingly threaten to beat the kids with it if they didn't behave. Gus knew she was probably kidding, but just to be on the safe side, he took the rubber hose and buried it deep in the garden.

About twenty years ago, Suzette Saint-Ours, of Mendon, New York, was leaving a humane society shelter when she saw some people carrying in an armful of twelve-week-old puppies they wanted to "get rid of."

Suzette spotted a buff-colored female among the litter of black-and-white pups and, she recalls, "Something just clicked between us." She named the puppy Honey. As the dog matured, she appeared to be mostly collie, with some golden retriever mixed in.

Suzette and Honey had seventeen mutually loving years together. As Honey advanced to her great age, she lost her hearing but was generally in fine shape and her sight remained fairly good. Toward the end of her long life, however, Honey frequently fell when walking and had to have human help to get back up on her feet.

By this time Suzette and her veterinarian husband, Laurel Kaddatz, also had Tippy. A Cairn terrier-plus, Tippy was about a year old when her owners brought her to Laurel's hospital to be put to sleep, claiming they'd been unable to housebreak her and that she had a destructive chewing habit. Dr. Kaddatz took Tippy into his own family, and she proved to be a delightful pet. She also became a source of real help to Honey.

Tippy appointed herself the old dog's guardian. Each time Honey fell down and was unable to rise, Tippy (who otherwise never barked) barked loudly until Suzette came and lifted Honey to her feet again. The system worked: Tippy seemed to recognize the problem and figured out how to get help to resolve it, and did so over and over again.

This exceptional little dog demonstrated a seeming ability to reason in another way. When Tippy's "security blanket" was dirty, she took it to the washing machine and left it in the pile of dirty clothes waiting to be washed.

As the stories in this chapter illustrate, some dogs do seem to have the capacity to create unique solutions to problems they encounter. For Zack, the German shepherd, to gently remove potentially dangerous sticks from small children (if you recall, he also removed the gun from a man's hand in Chapter Seven), and for Butch, the beagle, to tiptoe across a linoleum floor to circumvent the rules of the house appears to have no other explanation than an ability to reason.

Chapter 15

Reasoning Cats

*When I play with my cat, who knows whether I
do not make her more sport than she makes me?*
—Michel De Montaigne

Colonel Stuart Wortley had a cat that was wounded in
the Crimean War. Daily, he took the cat to the regimen-
tal surgeon to have the bayonet-wounded paw medi-
cated. Then the colonel got sick and was laid up for a
while. The story goes that the cat—all on her own—
calmly presented herself to the doctor each day for treatment.[1]

Cats are basically independent; their preference for
solitary living, as opposed to the highly socialized per-
sona of the dog, results in comparatively fewer observa-
tions about feline reasoning abilities. That cats have a
capacity to understand cause and effect is clearly demonstrated when they perform heroic feats (Chapter Nine).
There is no doubt that cats are highly intelligent. But
they do have their own unique ways of thinking.

Cats are creatures of habit, and they like routine.
That could explain the above story of Colonel Wortley's
cat, as well as the following story of Teddy, contributed
by Georgia Bender:

Ah, Teddy! Who knows what Teddy thinks? He is our
boy-in-a-cat-suit, a bulky, baggy cream with strange
ideas. Some cats imagine they are people. Teddy knows
better and carries that idea a step further. To Teddy,

people belong to cats and one person in particular is his. The house is also his.

Teddy supervises housekeeping and is a whiz at making beds. He knows the exact routine—what is pulled tight, what is pulled up—and walks about on the bed to each point at the right time. One morning the female human that does such things for him was a trifle late and entered the room to find him standing at the head of the bed pawing at the edge of the bottom sheet . . .

A charming story of a cat's recognition of cause and effect is that of Charles Dickens's cat, Williamina (originally named William, until her sex was established). Dickens enjoyed Williamina's presence on his lap while he worked late in his study. One night, the candle on his desk went out. He relit it, stroked the black cat a bit, and then went back to work. The light flickered again, and he looked up to see Williamina trying to snuff out the candle with her paw. She meowed at him and, tickled by her resourcefulness in getting his attention, he stopped working and petted her thoroughly.

Dottie Hilvers, of Cincinnati, Ohio, writes more about her cat Simon (mentioned in Chapter Three), who obviously had a way of figuring things out:

Simon knew where we kept the excess canned cat food—down in the basement in a cupboard with a lift-up latch. We'd catch him on the freezer next to it, pushing up the handle with his paw while our black cat, Bugs, was below opening the door and batting out a can of food and sinking his teeth in the paper label. When caught, Simon would act embarrassed and slink away.

As any cat owner can verify, cats are acutely sensitive to change; move a piece of furniture in the living room, and the resident cat will approach it with exaggerated suspicion. Cats also appear to be uncommonly aware of the shapes of objects. Georgia Bender contributes this captivating story:

Like so many who love animals, I have a collection of animal figurines, two favorites of which sit on my dresser. One has been there for twenty years and is a grouping of three white cats consisting of a mother flanked by kittens. Lovely and serene, they sit on a green base.

The other figurine has been there only a few months. It's a textured brown tabby with realistic eyes and a male aura.

One afternoon I turned and found Teddy, our large, beige plush cat (mentioned earlier in this chapter), standing on the dresser. As I watched, he tried to pick up the mother cat with kittens in his teeth. When I shouted at him, he stopped but cuffed the new tabby figurine before jumping down.

I have a petite, thoroughly enchanting, gray tiger cat named Rascal. I bought a wooden Santa Claus figure at a craft show last fall. The figure includes a small burlap sack filled with tiny toys. Poking out of the sack are candy canes, a Christmas tree, some fruit, and an extremely small mouse. The mouse is realistic looking, but it's obviously not a cat toy, and there's nothing soft or fuzzy about it.

On Christmas morning, I found the mouse on the floor, riddled with tiny teeth marks, its bedraggled condition proclaiming a night of terror. Rascal had carefully, and without disturbing the other delicate objects in the sack, selected her prey.

There is some debate over whether or not animals have a sense of humor, which is supposed to be another sign of true intelligence. Most pet owners can affirm their animals have this sense in full measure, and there are innumerable stories to back this up.

Georgia Bender, who has contributed numerous stories to this book, has had many pets over the years. As both a professional writer and a warm and keen observer of animals, she has the talent and inclination to write charming and interesting tales about their exploits. This next story is Georgia's:

Hide and seek. Many cats love it.

Our cat, Little Fellow, used to play it with my daughters, which usually strikes a pet owner as a sign of remarkable intelligence. Actually, any cat that could not find a child would have to be seriously deficient, for any child who imagines he or she is being silent is really rustling, stamping, giggling, whispering, and bumping into things.

The cat that comprehends the game so thoroughly as to hide in its turn is much rarer, but such was my mother's cat, Miss Purr, a long-haired tricolor with a classic harlequin face. I would hide behind a door or under a bed, and she would find me immediately. Then she would disappear, and finding her was much more difficult.

Her favorite hiding place, it turned out, was up inside the Philco radio console, which had a round hole in the bottom. We never would have found her out if Purr hadn't finally let her tail hang down through the hole.

Another cat, Oscar-She, not only played but also altered the game, for she had a nature as sunny as her color and a mind as blank as a summer day. She considered herself hidden if *she* could not see *us*. She would crouch before the sofa, head and shoulders underneath . . . and tail and rump in plain sight.

But it was no good to cry, "Oh, there's Oscar! I see you, dumb, old Oscar!" and grab her immediately, for she would be crushed. Even she knew that wasn't how the game should be played.

So hunting for Oscar-She became an elaborate game of its own, and even Mama and Gramma dropped everything to join in, all of us stomping around and remarking, "Have you seen Oscar-She?" Even Purr would come down out of the Philco to sit on the hearth and watch with disbelief.

All the while Oscar-She would get more and more excited, rump wiggling and tail twitching, until it seemed time for me to exclaim with wonder, "Oh, there's Oscar!" and then continue while cuddling her, "How did you ever think of hiding there, darling Oscar?"

And everyone was happy, especially Oscar-She.

Plainly, each and every cat has its own way of figuring things out. There are clever cats like Simon who know just how to solve a problem, and cats like Oscar-She who only think they know what's up (although Oscar-She's kind humans aided and abetted her in this self-delusion). There is always something interesting, if occasionally unfathomable, going on in a cat's mind.

Chapter 16

Other Examples of Reasoning

*Love the animals, love the plants, love every-
thing. If you love everything, you will
perceive the divine mystery in things.*
—Fyodor Dostoyevsky

As mentioned in Chapter Thirteen, the theory that only
the human animal can fashion and use tools no longer
holds water. Jane Goodall knocked the scientific world
on its ear when, in the course of her study of chim-
panzees in Tanzania, she observed the chimps stripping
leaves from twigs (thus modifying them into more effec-
tive tools), then carrying the twigs to termite mounds
where they inserted them to catch and eat termites.

The world was also amazed at the discovery that sea
otters use tools. These engaging creatures carry stones
beneath their armpits, and use the stones to pound shellfish open. They float on their backs to do this, pressing
the shell against their chests while hammering at it with
the stone. (Some observers claim the reverse method is
used: The otter places the stone on its chest and brings
the shellfish down hard on the stone until the shell
breaks open.) Sometimes they carry the stone underwat-
er to pry abalones from the ocean floor. They select
stones of the right size, and have been known to keep a
good one for a long time.

Supposedly, polar bears have been observed flinging
chunks of ice at seals, thereby injuring them enough to

be captured. And grizzly bears, as well as other hunted animals, are reported to craftily station themselves in spots which allow them to observe hunters, without themselves being seen. Furthermore, it is said that some grizzlies appear to go to great lengths to avoid leaving tracks, suggesting awareness that their tracks can lead hunters to them.[1]

There are verified reports of monkeys herding sheep and driving tractors. There are incredible stories about baboons, including the story of Jack, who responsibly operated railway signals by himself. And then there is Washoe, the chimpanzee who communicated intelligently with humans via sign language.

Certain water animals perform amazing feats which indicate a capacity to reason. In many animal books, for instance, documented stories appear about dolphins and whales attempting to lift an ill or injured companion to the water's surface to prevent its drowning.

Manatees (also known as sea cows) are large, peaceful, air-breathing mammals that eat aquatic plants in shallow beds along the coast of Florida. There are only about twelve hundred of these unique animals in the United States today, and they are an endangered species.

High-speed power boats are the main cause of mortality among manatees. Unlike other large water animals, manatees are vegetarians and graze in water only three to four feet deep. Because they've never had to develop the speed and maneuverability of predators, who have to catch their meals, manatees are sluggish in water and unable to dodge speeding boats.

Joe Kenner, Park Biologist at Blue Spring State Park in Orange City, Florida, was kind enough to permit the use of the following manatee story, which happened about ten years ago at Blue Spring.

Rangers at the park responded to a report of a dead manatee that, it turned out, had been struck by a power boat. When the rangers arrived on the scene, however, they detected some movement in the body, and thought perhaps the adult female had only been injured.

On closer examination, they found she was indeed dead. The movement of her body was the result of three other manatees—her calf and two adults—nudging her from below in an effort to raise her head above the surface of the water.

When the rangers hooked onto the dead manatee's body, the others registered alarm. They are gentle, thoroughly nonaggressive creatures, but one manatee conveyed its great distress by raising its head a good foot and a half out of the water and vocalizing. Normally, the rangers report, manatees seldom expose their heads above water to that degree, and the rasping squeal which serves as their vocalization had been heard only beneath water prior to that. The three manatees followed the body as it was towed, the calf remaining alongside its mother all the way to the loading ramp.

Whether domestic or wild, animals are capable of astonishing displays of reasoning. Some people have had intriguing experiences with wild animals that have become pets.

Jane Dickinson, a resident of Webster, New York, worked in her veterinarian husband's office. She recalls a story an elderly farm couple told her when they stopped by the office.

The couple, Jane remembers, had found a young woodchuck on their property and raised him as a pet. He had free run of their farmhouse and went in and out through a screen door on their back porch all during his first spring, summer, and early fall.

The woodchuck spent his winter hibernation undisturbed in a barn on their property. When he awoke in the second spring of his life he resumed his pet status, but he went outdoors more often and was gone for increasingly longer periods of time.

One day the woodchuck came in the house and approached the woman. He was excited and was able to convey to the woman that he wanted her to follow him. She did, and he led her outdoors. Waiting for him in the back yard was a young female woodchuck.

It seemed he wanted his human to meet his mate. He ran back and forth between the woman and the female woodchuck, demonstrating as clearly as if he could talk that he was torn between his human and his own kind.

Nature won the battle, of course, and he left for good with his mate. But at least he showed the woman why he had to leave her now. Although she appreciated it, it struck her as a curious and amazing gesture of explanation and good-bye.

Woodchucks, or groundhogs, are marmots and are found in Canada and the eastern United States. The most famous woodchuck is Pennsylvania's Punxsutawney Phil, who "predicts" six more weeks of winter if he comes out of his burrow and sees his shadow on February 2 of every year.

Woodchucks are considered nuisance animals and are avidly hunted. I have to admit even I became exasperated one day when I plunged into five different woodchuck holes as I pruned trees in our orchard. I fell into the large and conspicuous burrow openings (I don't claim to be observant), but their hidden, or "blind," holes are much more dangerous—livestock can step into them and break a leg.

Woodchucks, holes aside, are sanitary and appealing animals. They are one of the few animals other than the dog to wag their tails in friendly greeting (foxes and prairie dogs are two others).* And pet woodchucks, like cats, sometimes purr with contentment, as do pet squirrels and raccoons.[2] John James Audubon, the naturalist, had a pet woodchuck which slept on the hearth and had an amiable relationship with his dog and cat.[3]

In nature, the disbanding of the growing woodchuck family occurs in stages. Unlike many other animals, the

---

* In his books *Catwatching* and *Dogwatching*, Desmond Morris promotes the theory that animals wag their tails when experiencing conflict, and that seems likely in these cases, also; although too lengthy to go into here, the circumstances in which the above wag their tails would indicate both friendliness and apprehension.

young are not simply driven from home and tossed out into the cold, cruel world to fend for themselves when the burrow becomes overcrowded.

The young move into abandoned burrows close by the mother's burrow (she digs new ones for them if no empties are available), and she keeps a protective eye on them. The mother visits the young chucks daily when they first leave home, and then slowly gives them more independence. The young woodchucks gradually leave the territory and get on with their lives.[4]

Could it have been the innate acknowledgment of family concern that caused the woodchuck in the above story to feel he should explain his leaving?

It's fascinating how some pets feel compelled to stop other pets from doing things which upset their humans. Our own cats scratched the furniture, naturally, before we saw the light and bought that more-precious-than-gold necessity: a floor-to-ceiling cat post.

Cowgirl, my Australian shepherd, saw we were bothered when our upholstery was shredded, and she took it upon herself to stop the cats. As soon as Cowgirl heard the plucking of fabric, she ran to the cats and pushed them away from the furniture—not just occasionally, but every single time. She was a real help.

The cats got so they'd sit beside the couch, stretch out a paw to hook into the upholstery, pause, glance at Cowgirl, and walk away. When we installed the multi-level scratching post the cats immediately began clawing it to pieces, but Cowgirl paid no attention. If they returned to damaging the furniture, however, she interfered. She knew the difference.

Georgia Bender, of Kittanning, Pennsylvania, writes of her five-year-old, small tabby-and-white cat Suzy, who shares her humans with their other cat, Teddy:

> Suzy's specialty is opening doors. For most of us, doors open in two ways, push and pull, and Suzy has mastered those with ease.

Her favorite door, the one she is proudest of opening, is the little door in the base of the gun cabinet. It stays shut because a key turns a small metal bar inside. Thus it is neither a push nor a pull door, for the key must be turned.

Suzy performs this feat in a noisy game of sitting up and batting at the door with both fists, until she eventually knocks the key and the door swings open. Bang, bang, bang, bang . . . she can be heard all over the house until we start yelling, "Suzy! Stop it!" And Teddy runs in and hits her.

Cats' sensitivity to the shapes of objects was discussed in Chapter Fifteen, but the reactions of animals in general to images and shapes is a fascinating topic. Some animals identify and respond to all sorts of inanimate objects.

Alexander the Great's favorite horse was named Bucephalus, a black stallion considered untamable at the time twelve-year-old Alexander tamed him. No one else ever rode him, and Alexander would ride no horse into battle other than Bucephalus. Bucephalus died of exhaustion during the battle of the Hydaspes, and Alexander thought so highly of the horse he named a conquered town (Buchephala) in his honor.[5]

At one point, Alexander had his portrait painted astride his favorite horse. Upon completion, he felt the artist hadn't painted the magnificent stallion realistically. In self-defense, the artist had Bucephalus brought to view the painting. The horse took one look and neighed at the image, winning the argument in favor of the artist.[6]

I've noticed that animals react to their mirror images and to television sights and sounds when very young, but tend to become indifferent as they get older.

Not all animals ignore them, however. Barbara Milliken's television-watching Burmese has already been mentioned in Chapter Six. And Margaret Yarbrough, of

Auburn, Alabama, had a dachshund they called Hot Shot (registered name Lady Veronica Vonn Devereux) who adored fetching thrown balls in real life, and became addicted to televised ball games. Margaret writes:

> If the pitcher threw a strike, Hot Shot thought she could find it in the room and bring the ball back to him. If he threw to first base, she ran to the side of the TV to see if the ball was on the floor. The batters hitting a ball didn't excite her. It was the pitcher throwing straight to her that made Hot Shot think he was playing ball with her, and that she was supposed to bring the ball back to him. She could last through extra innings, and it was as much fun watching her as the major league teams.

Jeanne Huenefeld, of Cincinnati, Ohio, writes of her politically-savvy, one-eyed black cat Jackson:

> Jackson is the light of my life, and I'll accept anyone's impression of me as completely crazy where he is concerned. Example: When the debates for the presidential election were on TV, Jackson sat on the footrest of my recliner chair and watched intently. We giggled because it is not his habit to look at the television screen unless there's an educational picture about birds in flight. But he seemed to enjoy the voices of the candidates.

> After the program was over, he'd turn around to me as if to determine my choice between the two men. Just to be humorous I'd say, "Jackson, if you want Dukakis, jump down and go to the left, and if you want Bush, go to the right." He *always* went to the right. We'd laugh over this and tell it to our friends.

> I liked Dukakis right from the start when nobody seemed to have heard of him. But right up until voting day, Jackson held his Republican view. I voted for Bush and let it be known that there was no way I was going to doubt the intelligence of my cat.

Jackson no longer watches TV, since all the political stuff has ceased—and he takes turns jumping off the chair either to the right or the left, whatever suits his fancy. But he never varied in his position before the election.

The last story in the book was told to me by Mary Barnes of Clyde, New York. Although it's a small story, it packs a big message.

Mary and her husband Jim stopped at a supermarket one evening last fall to pick up a few items. Jim ran in to get them, while Mary waited in the pickup.

There are several Amish families in the area who also shop at this store. They leave their horses and buggies tied to a lamp post near the road, beyond the parked cars. An Amish family was there that evening.

Mary, who has always owned and loved horses, was watching the buggy horse, a bay gelding who stood with one leg cocked, patiently waiting. Suddenly he raised his head, looked toward the store, and whinnied. Mary followed his gaze and saw the Amish family in their straw hats and drab clothes passing by the large front window on their way to the checkout.

As the family came out of the store, the horse nickered again, in welcome.

"It was nice, and it made you stop and think," says Mary. "Here everyone else was coming back to cold chrome and steel, but they were returning to something that *cared*."

Glossary

BITCH — A female dog.

BURROW — A tunnel or hole dug in the ground by an animal, used for shelter or refuge.

CANTER — A smooth, easy gait, similar to a collected gallop; lope.

COLT — A male horse less than four years old.

CROSS — A mix of breeds, when referring to a dog.

EUTHANIZE — To "put to sleep"; the administration of a lethal injection by a veterinarian to end an animal's suffering.

FERAL — Wild.

FOAL — A baby horse.

GELDING — A castrated male horse.

HAND — The measurement used to determine the size of a horse. A hand is equal to four inches. A horse 15 hands, two inches (15:2) would be 62 inches from the top of its withers to the ground. If under 14:2 hands (58 inches), the animal is considered a pony.

HERBIVORE — An animal that feeds mainly on grasses and plants; vegetarian.

HERPETOLOGIST — An expert on reptiles and amphibians.

HIBERNATE — To pass the winter in a dormant state.

IN-AND-OUTER — A term used to describe cats who are allowed freedom of choice to be either indoors or outdoors.

INSTINCT — An inborn tendancy to behave in certain ways common to the species.

MARE — A female horse over age four; younger than four is a filly.

MARMOT — A burrowing rodent (rodents are simply animals that gnaw) with a short, bushy tail and coarse fur.

NESTLING — A very young bird, not yet able to leave the nest.

PACER — Standardbred racehorses are classified as either trotters or pacers. Pacers perform a two-beat gait, with the lateral legs moving together.

SPAY/NEUTER — To surgically alter an animal so that it is unable to breed or bear young.

STALLION — A mature, intact (uncastrated) male horse.

STRAY — A homeless animal.

SULKY — A two-wheeled, lightweight, one-horse carriage with room to carry only one person, used in harness racing.

SUPERNATURAL — Something outside the normal experience or knowledge of humans; unexplainable by the known laws of nature.

TABBY — A gray, brown, yellow or reddish-orange cat with darker stripes. Also sometimes referred to as "tiger."

TOM CAT — An intact (unneutered) male.

TORTOISE-SHELL or TORTIE — Evenly distributed patches of red (orangeish-red), black, and cream colors. If the tortie has white on its face, chest, and legs it is called calico. Calico and tortoise-shell cats are almost always female.

TRICOLOR — Having three colors in the coat, usually white, black, and brown.

Endnotes

CHAPTER 1

1. Thelma Wible, "Ghost Dogs in Lore and Legend," *Dog Fancy*, October 1985, p. 47.
2. Bill Schul, *The Psychic Power of Animals* (Greenwich, CT: Fawcett Publications, Inc., 1977), p. 113.
3. Earl of Carnarvon, *Memoirs of the Earl of Carnarvon* (London: Weidenfeld and Nicolson, 1976), pp. 125-127.
4. Ann Hornaday, *Matters of Fact: Cats & Cat Lovers* (Stamford, CT: Longmeadow Press, 1988), p. 39.

CHAPTER 2

1. Alton A. Lindsey, *The Bicentennial of John James Audubon* (Bloomington: Indiana University Press, 1985), pp. 85-86.
2. Maurice Burton, *The Sixth Sense of Animals* (New York: Taplinger Publishing Company, 1973), p. 30.

CHAPTER 3

1. Burton, *The Sixth Sense of Animals*, p. 138.
2. Gerald L. Wood, *Animal Facts and Feats: A Guinness Record of the Animal Kingdom* (London: Guinness Superlatives LTD, 1982), p. 159.
3. Katherine A. Houpt, V.M.D., Ph.D. and Thomas R. Wolski, D.V.M., *Domestic Animal Behavior for*

Veterinarians and Animal Scientists (Ames, IA: The Iowa State University Press, 1982), p. 178.

4. Elinor DeWire, "Cats at Sea," *Cat Fancy*, March 1988, pp. 44-45.

CHAPTER 4

1. Elinor Goulding Smith, *Horses, History and Havoc* (New York: The World Publishing Company, 1969), p. 180.
2. Maurice Burton, *Just Like an Animal* (New York: Charles Scribner's Sons, 1978), p. 81.

CHAPTER 5

1. Julien Green, *God's Fool: The Life and Times of Francis of Assisi*, trans. Peter Heinegg (San Francisco: Harper & Row, 1985), pp. 218-219.
2. Ibid., p. 271.
3. Roger A. Caras, *A Celebration of Cats* (New York: Simon and Schuster, 1986), p. 136.
4. Adam Zamoyski, *Paderewski* (New York: Atheneum 1982), p. 37.
5. Laura Benét, *Enchanting Jenny Lind* (New York: Dodd, Mead & Company, 1964), pp. 11-15.
6. M. Oldfield Howey, *The Horse in Magic and Myth* (London: William Rider & Son LTD, 1923), pp. 156-157.

CHAPTER 6

1. John C. Ewers, *The Horse in Blackfoot Indian Culture* (Washington: GPO, 1955), pp. 196, 257-259, 283-287, 290-291, 326.

CHAPTER 7

1. Wible, "Ghost Dogs in Lore and Legend," p. 47.
2. Joseph Wylder, *Psychic Pets: The Secret World of Animals* (New York: Perennial Library-Harper & Row Publishers, 1979), pp. 71-72.
3. C.G.E. Wimhurst, *The Complete Book of Toy Dogs* (New York: G.P. Putnam's Sons, 1969), pp. 204-205.

4. Ibid., p. 177.
5. Wible, "Ghost Dogs in Lore and Legend," p. 49.

CHAPTER 8

1. Kit and George Harrison, *America's Favorite Backyard Wildlife* (New York: Simon and Schuster, 1985), pp. 190-191.

CHAPTER 9

1. Loren Spiotta-DiMare, "The Sassy Siamese," *Cat Fancy*, March 1987, p. 36.
2. Jo Manton and Robert Gittings, *The Flying Horses: Tales from China* (New York: Holt, Rinehart and Winston, 1977), pp. 156-158.
3. Hornaday, *Matters of Fact: Cats & Cat Lovers*, p. 31.
4. Houpt and Wolski, *Domestic Animal Behavior for Veterinarians and Animal Scientists*, p. 245.

CHAPTER 10

1. Margaret Cabell Self, *The Horseman's Encyclopedia,* new and rev. ed. (New York: A.S. Barnes and Company, Inc., 1963), p. 104.
2. Douglas Southall Freeman, *R.E. Lee: A Biography,* 4 vols. (New York: Charles Scribner's Sons, 1963), vol. 1, pp. 615, 645.
3. Ibid., vol. 3, p. 320.

CHAPTER 11

1. Edward Wagenknecht, *Edgar Allan Poe: The Man Behind the Legend* (New York: Oxford University Press, 1963), p. 64.
2. Wimhurst, *The Complete Book of Toy Dogs*, p. 156.
3. Lindsey, *The Bicentennial of John James Audubon*, pp. 99-100.
4. P. Ansell Robin, *Animal Lore in English Literature* (London: John Murray, 1932), pp. 65-67.
5. Ibid., pp. 63-64.

CHAPTER 13

1. Robin, *Animal Lore In English Literature*, pp. 166-167.
2. Ibid., p. 167.
3. Donald R. Griffin, *Animal Thinking* (Cambridge: Harvard University Press, 1984), pp. 36, 88-91.
4. "Hives Found by Hunters who Follow Wild Birds," Rochester (NY) *Democrat & Chronicle*, March 11, 1989, p. 4B.
5. Griffin, *Animal Thinking*, pp. 127-128.
6. James Roland, "Experts Disagree Over What's Poisoning Herons," *Sarasota Herald Tribune*, June 12, 1989, pp. 1B, 4B.

CHAPTER 14

1. Dr. H. Hediger, *The Psychology and Behaviour of Animals in Zoos and Circuses*, trans. Geoffrey Sircom (New York: Dover Publications, Inc., 1968), pp. 16, 19.
2. Francis Russell, *The Shadow of Blooming Grove: Warren G. Harding in His Times* (New York: McGraw-Hill Book Company, 1968), p. 444.

CHAPTER 15

1. John Beecroft, ed., *Plain and Fancy Cats* (New York: Rhinehart & Company, Inc., 1958), p. 207.

CHAPTER 16

1. Griffin, *Animal Thinking*, pp. 74, 124.
2. Harrison, *America's Favorite Backyard Wildlife*, pp. 69, 209.
3. Robert Snedigar, *Our Small Native Animals: Their Habits and Care* (New York: Dover Publications, Inc., 1963), p. 41.
4. Harrison, *America's Favorite Backyard Wildlife*, pp. 210-212.
5. Charles Mercer, *Alexander The Great* (New York: Horizon Caravel-American Heritage Publishing Company, 1962), pp. 12, 16, 18, 99, 134.
6. Burton, *Just Like an Animal*, p. 183.

Bibliography of Sources

Albrecht, Steven. "A Look at Famous Cat Lovers." *CATS Magazine*, Oct. 1988, pp. 10, 12.

Amory, Cleveland. *The Cat Who Came for Christmas*. New York: Penguin Books, 1988.

Andriese, Pamela D., comp. *Proceedings of Conference XI: Abnormal Animal Behavior Prior to Earthquakes, II*. Convened Under Auspices of National Earthquake Hazards Reduction Program. United States Department of the Interior Geological Survey. Menlo Park, CA: GPO, 1980.

Anonymous Nineteenth-Century Sportsman. "A Gentleman's Dogs." *The Dog Book*. Jerrold Mundis, ed. New York: Arbor House, 1983.

Bartlett, John. *Bartlett's Familiar Quotations*. Boston: Little, Brown and Company, 1955.

Battle, Kemp P., comp. *Great American Folklore*. Garden City, NY: Doubleday & Company, Inc., 1986.

Beecroft, John, ed. *Plain and Fancy Cats*. New York: Rhinehart & Company, Inc., 1958.

Benét, Laura. *Enchanting Jenny Lind*. New York: Dodd, Mead & Company, 1964.

Breland, Osmond P. *Animal Life and Lore*. New York: Harper & Row, 1963.

Brown, Margaret Wise. *When the Wind Blew*. New York: Random House, 1979.

Burns, James MacGregor. *Roosevelt: The Soldier of Freedom*. New York: Harcourt Brace Jovanovich, Inc., 1970.

Burton, Maurice. *Just Like an Animal*. New York: Charles Scribner's Sons, 1978.

_____. *The Sixth Sense of Animals*. New York: Taplinger Publishing Company, 1973.

Burton, Robert. *Animal Senses*. New York: Taplinger Publishing Company, 1970.

Caras, Roger A. *A Celebration of Cats*. New York: Simon and Schuster, 1986.

Carnarvon, Earl of. *Memoirs of the Earl of Carnarvon*. London: Weidenfeld & Nicolson, 1976.

_____. *Ermine Tales: More Memoirs of the Earl of Carnarvon*. London: Weidenfeld & Nicolson, 1980.

Colette. "The Long Cat." *Plain and Fancy Cats*. John Beecroft, ed. New York: Rhinehart & Company, Inc., 1958.

Corbo, Margarete Sigl and Diane Marie Barras. *Arnie the Darling Starling*. Boston: Houghton Mifflin Company, 1983.

Corey, Paul. *Do Cats Think?* Secaucus, NJ: Castle, 1977.

De Wire, Elinor. "Cats at Sea." *Cat Fancy*, March 1988, pp. 42-45.

Droscher, Vitus B. *The Mysterious Senses of Animals*. New York: E.P. Dutton & Company, Inc., 1965.

Evans, Job Michael. "Presidential Pets." *Dog World*, April 1985, pp. 18, 50-51.

Ewers, John C. *The Horse in Blackfoot Indian Culture*. Washington: GPO, 1955.

Frankenberg, Robert, ed. *Cherokee Animal Tales*. New York: Holiday House, Inc., 1968.

Freeman, Douglas Southall. *R.E. Lee: A Biography.* 4 vols. New York: Charles Scribner's Sons, 1963.

Gaddis, Vincent and Margaret. *The Strange World of Animals and Pets.* New York: Cowles Book Company, Inc., 1970.

Green, Julien. *God's Fool: The Life and Times of Francis of Assisi.* Trans. Peter Heinegg. San Francisco: Harper & Row, 1985.

Greene, David. *Your Incredible Cat.* Garden City, NY: Doubleday & Company, 1986.

Griffin, Donald R. *Animal Thinking.* Cambridge: Harvard University Press, 1984.

_____. *The Question of Animal Awareness: Evolutionary Continuity of Mental Experience.* Los Altos, CA: William Kaufmann, Inc., 1981.

Harrison, Kit and George. *America's Favorite Backyard Wildlife.* New York: Simon and Schuster,1985.

Hearst Corporation. *Maneaters and Marmosets: Strange and Fascinating Tales from the Animal Kingdom.* New York: Hearst Books, 1976.

Hediger, Dr. H. *The Psychology and Behaviour of Animals in Zoos and Circuses.* Trans. Geoffrey Sircom. New York: Dover Publications, Inc., 1968.

"Hives Found by Hunters who Follow Wild Birds." *Democrat & Chronicle* (Rochester, NY), 11 March 1989, p. 4B.

Hornaday, Ann. *Matters of Fact: Cats & Cat Lovers.* Stamford, CT: Longmeadow Press, 1988.

Hotchner, A. E. *Papa Hemingway: A Personal Memoir.* New York: Random House, 1966.

Houpt, Katherine A. and Thomas R. Wolski. *Domestic Animal Behavior for Veterinarians and Animal Scientists.* Ames, IA: The Iowa State University Press, 1982.

Howey, M. Oldfield. *The Horse in Magic and Myth.* London: William Rider & Son LTD, 1923.

Kipling, Rudyard. *Rudyard Kipling's Verse: Definitive Edition*. Garden City, NY: Doubleday & Company, Inc., 1940.

Knight, Eric. *Lassie-Come-Home*. New York: Holt, Rinehart & Winston, 1968.

Lattimore, Richmond, trans. *The Iliad of Homer*. Chicago: The University of Chicago Press, 1951.

Lindsey, Alton A. *The Bicentennial of John James Audubon*. Bloomington: Indiana University Press, 1985.

Lintner, Anita. "The Mysterious Cat." *Cat Fancy*, Oct. 1988, pp. 21-22.

MacGregor, Alastair. *Cat Calls*. New York: E.P. Dutton, 1988.

Manton, Jo and Robert Gittings. *The Flying Horses: Tales from China*. New York: Holt, Rinehart & Winston, 1977.

Mathews, L. Harrison and Maxwell Knight. *The Senses of Animals*. London: Museum Press LTD, 1963.

Mercer, Charles. *Alexander The Great*. New York: Horizon Caravel-American Heritage Publishing Company, 1962.

Mockler, Anthony. *Francis of Assisi: The Wandering Years*. Oxford: Phaidon Press LTD, 1976.

Morris, Desmond. *Catwatching*. New York: Crown Publishers, Inc., 1986.

_____. *Dogwatching*. New York: Crown Publishers, Inc., 1987.

_____. *The Human Zoo*. New York: McGraw-Hill Book Company, 1969.

Munroe, David Hoadly. *The Grand National: 1839-1930*. New York: Huntington Press, 1931.

Packard, Vance. *Animal IQ: The Human Side of Animals*. New York: The Dial Press, 1950.

Peare, Catherine Owens. *The FDR Story*. New York: Thomas Y. Crowell Company, 1962.

Raymond, Meredith B. and Mary Rose Sullivan, eds. *Women of Letters: Selected Letters of Elizabeth Barrett Browning & Mary Russell Mitford*. Boston: Twayne Publishers, 1987.

Rhine, J. B. and Sara R. Feather. "The Study of Cases of Psi-Trailing in Animals." *Journal of Parapsychology*, vol. 26, No. 1 (March, 1962): pp. 1-22.

Robin, P. Ansell. *Animal Lore in English Literature*. London: John Murray, 1932.

Roland, James. "Experts Disagree Over What's Poisoning Herons." *Sarasota Herald Tribune*, 12 June 1989, pp. 1B,4B.

Russell, Francis. *The Shadow of Blooming Grove: Warren G. Harding in His Times*. New York: McGraw-Hill Book Company, 1968.

Schul, Bill. *The Psychic Power of Animals*. Greenwich, CT: Fawcett Publications, Inc., 1977.

Self, Margaret Cabell. *The Horseman's Encyclopedia: New and Revised Edition*. New York: A.S. Barnes & Company, Inc, 1963.

Sewell, Anna. *Black Beauty*. Adapted by Eleanor Graham Vance. New York: Random House, 1949.

Smith, Bradley. *The Horse in the West*. New York: The World Publishing Company, 1972.

Smith, Elinor Goulding. *Horses, History and Havoc*. New York: The World Pulbishing Company, 1969.

Smythe, R.H. *Animal Psychology*. Springfield, IL: Charles C. Thomas, 1961.

Snedigar, Robert. *Our Small Native Animals: Their Habits and Care*. New York: Dover Publications, Inc., 1963.

Spiotta-DiMare, Loren. "The Sassy Siamese." *Cat Fancy*, March 1987, pp. 36-41.

Steeh, Judith A. *The Complete Book of Cats*. Greenwich, CT: Bison Books Corp., 1978.

Steinkraus, William C. and M. A. Stoneridge. *The Horse in Sport*. New York: Stewart, Tabori & Chang, 1987.

Stern, Philip Van Doren, ed. *Edgar Allan Poe*. New York: Penguin Books, 1984.

Thomas, Bill. *Talking with the Animals*. New York: William Morrow & Company, Inc., 1985.

Tributsch, Helmut. *When the Snakes Awake: Animals and Earthquake Prediction*. Trans. Paul Langner. Cambridge: The MIT Press, 1982.

Wagenknecht, Edward. *Edgar Allan Poe: The Man Behind the Legend*. New York: Oxford University Press, 1963.

White, Betty with Thomas J. Watson. *Pet Love: How Pets Take Care of Us*. New York: Pinnacle Books, 1983.

Wible, Thelma. "Ghost Dogs in Lore and Legend." *Dog Fancy*, Oct. 1985, pp. 47-49.

Wimhurst, C.G.E. *The Complete Book of Toy Dogs*. New York: G.P. Putnam's Sons, 1969.

Wood, Gerald L. *Animal Facts and Feats: A Guinness Record of the Animal Kingdom*. London: Guinness Superlatives LTD, 1982.

Woolf, Virginia. *Flush: A Biography*. New York: Harcourt, Brace & World, Inc., 1961.

Wylder, Joseph. *Psychic Pets: The Secret World of Animals*. New York: Perennial Library-Harper & Row Publishers, 1979.

Zamoyski, Adam. *Paderewski*. New York: Atheneum, 1982.

Index